Linda Hoyt and Teresa Therriault

Mastering *the* Mechanics

Ready-to-Use Lessons for Modeled, Guided, and Independent Editing

**SCHOLASTIC**

NEW YORK • TORONTO • LONDON • AUCKLAND • SYDNEY
MEXICO CITY • NEW DELHI • HONG KONG • BUENOS AIRES

Credits
Ruth Culham's Copy Editor's Symbols

Cover design by Jay Namerow
Interior design by Maria Lilja
Interior photos by Linda Hoyt, Teresa Therriault, and Patrick Burke
Acquiring editor: Lois Bridges
Production editor: Erin K. L. Grelak
Copy Editor: David Klein
ISBN 13: 978-0-545-04879-8
ISBN 10: 0-545-04879-6

We dedicate this to our husbands, Steve and Darrel. They make us smile, support us in countless ways, and love to remind us how lucky we are to have their love and support. They are right. We are wonderfully lucky to have them. Thanks, guys!

ACKNOWLEDGMENTS

We feel fortunate to have worked together for many years as Title I teachers, staff developers, and friends. Through these years, we have had many mentors who have helped us lift our practice, challenge our thinking, and find the courage to reach beyond what we knew yesterday. Those mentors include our colleagues, each other, the children we have had the honor to serve, and those powerful professionals whose books on writing constantly challenge and inform us. Donald Graves, Donald Murray, Shelley Harwayne, Lucy Calkins, Regie Routman, Ralph Fletcher, Katie Wood Ray, and many others have carried the torch and helped us all make a bigger difference for young writers. A special thanks to our local mentor, Ruth Culham, who has graciously allowed us to utilize her chart on copyediting symbols.

At Kinnaman Elementary in Beaverton, Oregon, Jan McCall, principal, opened her heart and the classrooms of her wonderful learning community so that we could capture the photos that appear in this resource and on the cover. Led by Marie Davis, Melissa Suesserman, Angie Thomas, Heidi Cochran, Traci Orth, and Patty Jo Foley, these beautiful children stretched our thinking and confirmed the validity of these cycles.

The lessons in this resource were carefully tested to ensure they were classroom-ready and reflective of the challenges young editors face. Piloting educators included district administrators, teachers, principals, and consultants. Their feedback to the learning cycles put muscle behind our thinking through their insightful observations of learners and helpful suggestions. In Davidson County, North Carolina, our heartfelt thanks go to Sonja Parks, April Willard, Wendy Younts, Leigh Ann Bruff, Amber Idol, Amber Parker, Stephanie Ward, and Tricia Prevette. In Ukiah, California, we thank Kathryn McInnis, Debbee Freeman, Cathy Hessom, Gayle Kline, Janet McLeod, Caryl Mastrof, and Leslie Maricle-Barclay for opening their thinking and classrooms to engage with the lessons. Kelly Boswell and Barbara Coleman, master teachers and independent consultants, provided valuable affirmations and encouragement. Lynnette Brent, Linda's trusted pen pal and friend, shared her creative thinking in the Pulling It All Together lessons and shared her editorial expertise in the lesson cycles.

We have found it quite joyous to get to know the team at Scholastic. Lois Bridges, our amazing editor and trusted friend, is a cherished anchor, always smoothing the way with careful suggestions, time-saving support, and unflagging optimism. Gloria Pipkin, our eagle-eyed "Grammar Goddess," helped us check and recheck the validity of our grammar lessons and skills continuum. We loved our tips from Miss Thistlebottom! Terry Cooper, Ray Coutu, David Klein, Maria Lilja, and Erin K. L. Grelak have generously shared their thinking, expanded our vision, and helped this resource take shape in the teacher-friendly manner we so wished to achieve. It has been a pleasure, and we thank them sincerely.

TABLE OF CONTENTS

To print out the reproducibles at full size in the Tools, Assessment and Record Keeping, and Appendix: Student Writing Samples sections, please visit www.scholastic.com/masteringthemechanics.

Introduction: Mastering the Mechanics

Putting Editing in Perspective

We care about the conventions of written language and we are not alone. The parents of the students we serve, the community, and the public all care about and expect children to show growing expertise in the conventions of written language; to present written work in such a way that it is legible, is spelled correctly and that it demonstrates correct grammar, capitalization, and punctuation.

As we focus students on mechanics and conventions, we want to be very clear about our goals:

1. To nurture writers who understand that rich, well-crafted messages are their first and most important focus.

2. To help children understand that a study of mechanics and conventions is about *adding tools* that enhance our messages, not just about correcting and being "right."

It is important to state that we are not in favor of prepackaged programs that cast editing and conventions as "mistakes" or exercises in correction. These programs have very little embedded instruction and consistently overwhelm students with sentences that are so laden with errors that meaning is easily lost, leaving a writer with few connections to his or her own work.

> **Just as the baker who creates a cake from scratch takes pride in adding butter-cream roses atop chocolate swirls, students must learn to delight in knowing how to add the important touches of correct spelling, grammar, and punctuation.**
> —*Shelley Harwayne*

conventions
(spacing, handwriting, spelling, and grammar)

mechanics
(periods, capital letters, and so on)

Above all, as we cast attention upon mechanics and conventions, we must be sure that creative thinking flourishes during drafting and revision. If mechanics and editing are overemphasized, they can have the negative effect of reducing writing volume, causing students to limit their writing to words they are able to spell correctly or to use overly simplistic sentence structures.

Recast Mechanics and Conventions as Tools to Lift Writing Quality

Writers must understand that mechanics are not tedious obligations. They are tools that add clarity and interest to our writing. Carefully crafted modeled writing lessons improve craft, mechanics, grammar, and spelling. Our goal is to develop the understanding that writers integrate conventions into craft rather than seeing them simply as elements of "correctness." Modeled writing with a think-aloud recasting mechanics as craft might sound like this:

I want to write about how quiet it was when I was walking in the woods.
I could say: "I went walking in the woods. It was quiet." That is okay, but if
I think about how punctuation can help me write in more interesting ways,
I think I can make it even better.

What do you think of: "Shhh! Listen. . . As my feet crunch softly on the gravel path, the sound seems huge. It is so quiet in the forest that my footsteps sound loud!" Look how I used exclamation points and an ellipsis. These punctuation marks helped make my opening and my ending more interesting. And do you see the comma I used? The comma told my reader to take a little breath so the ending of my sentence is more dramatic. Using punctuation makes my writing better!

It is our sincere hope that this resource will help educators and children alike see conventions and mechanics through new eyes. We believe conventions and mechanics are naturally woven into the writing process at two major points:

1. During drafting: Conventions and mechanics support our messages and enhance communication. Carefully chosen punctuation can clarify, control volume and flow, plus make ideas sparkle!

2. During editing: Conventions and mechanics provide readers with access to our thinking. Correct spelling, grammar, spacing, and punctuation make our work accessible to readers.

PART I

Introduction: Mastering the Mechanics

Putting Editing in Perspective

We care about the conventions of written language and we are not alone. The parents of the students we serve, the community, and the public all care about and expect children to show growing expertise in the conventions of written language; to present written work in such a way that it is legible, is spelled correctly and that it demonstrates correct grammar, capitalization, and punctuation.

As we focus students on mechanics and conventions, we want to be very clear about our goals:

1. To nurture writers who understand that rich, well-crafted messages are their first and most important focus.

2. To help children understand that a study of mechanics and conventions is about *adding tools* that enhance our messages, not just about correcting and being "right."

It is important to state that we are not in favor of prepackaged programs that cast editing and conventions as "mistakes" or exercises in correction. These programs have very little embedded instruction and consistently overwhelm students with sentences that are so laden with errors that meaning is easily lost, leaving a writer with few connections to his or her own work.

> **❚❚** Just as the baker who creates a cake from scratch takes pride in adding buttercream roses atop chocolate swirls, students must learn to delight in knowing how to add the important touches of correct spelling, grammar, and punctuation. **❚❚**
> —*Shelley Harwayne*

conventions
(spacing, handwriting, spelling, and grammar)

mechanics
(periods, capital letters, and so on)

Above all, as we cast attention upon mechanics and conventions, we must be sure that creative thinking flourishes during drafting and revision. If mechanics and editing are overemphasized, they can have the negative effect of reducing writing volume, causing students to limit their writing to words they are able to spell correctly or to use overly simplistic sentence structures.

Recast Mechanics and Conventions as Tools to Lift Writing Quality

Writers must understand that mechanics are not tedious obligations. They are tools that add clarity and interest to our writing. Carefully crafted modeled writing lessons improve craft, mechanics, grammar, and spelling. Our goal is to develop the understanding that writers integrate conventions into craft rather than seeing them simply as elements of "correctness." Modeled writing with a think-aloud recasting mechanics as craft might sound like this:

I want to write about how quiet it was when I was walking in the woods.
I could say: "I went walking in the woods. It was quiet." That is okay, but if
I think about how punctuation can help me write in more interesting ways,
I think I can make it even better.

What do you think of: "Shhh! Listen... As my feet crunch softly on the gravel path, the sound seems huge. It is so quiet in the forest that my footsteps sound loud!" Look how I used exclamation points and an ellipsis. These punctuation marks helped make my opening and my ending more interesting. And do you see the comma I used? The comma told my reader to take a little breath so the ending of my sentence is more dramatic. Using punctuation makes my writing better!

It is our sincere hope that this resource will help educators and children alike see conventions and mechanics through new eyes. We believe conventions and mechanics are naturally woven into the writing process at two major points:

1. During drafting: Conventions and mechanics support our messages and enhance communication. Carefully chosen punctuation can clarify, control volume and flow, plus make ideas sparkle!

2. During editing: Conventions and mechanics provide readers with access to our thinking. Correct spelling, grammar, spacing, and punctuation make our work accessible to readers.

Steep Conventions in Meaning

We believe that we must keep the focus on meaning while steeping learners in conventions and mechanics. With this emphasis, it would be perfectly natural to have a modeled writing that looks and sounds something like:

> I love popcorn. I love the crackly crunch and poppety pop as kernels start to explode. One of the things I love is that the "pop" sometimes surprises me. I am going to use exclamation marks to show that in my writing. Watch to see how I use exclamation marks to make my meaning more precise. I add the exclamation mark {!} so the reader knows it was a quick burst of sound.

> "Pop! Pop! Poppety! I can hardly wait for those salty, crunchy bits to land on my tongue."

By recasting punctuation as a tool that can make our writing sparkle, we have maintained a clear focus on meaning. This kind of work on mechanics and conventions enriches communication and elevates writing quality.

Tiptoe Lightly With "Correctness"

We must avoid a situation where the fear of being incorrect freezes writers and forces them into a narrow zone of "correctness." In this kind of setting, writers can sometimes place too much emphasis on spelling, for example, and begin to limit their writing to words they know they can spell correctly. This dangerously limits the writing to the confines of spelling rather than letting it flourish through the writer's sense of language and imagination. While empowering writers with conventions, we must also take seriously our mission to keep meaning as the primary objective. Our goal: Language is lifted and elaborated with mechanics as a subset of the message.

> Conventions and mechanics should support meaning, not limit it.

Have High Expectations

We do believe, however, that it is appropriate to set expectations and to make it clear to students that after completing a cycle, they have new tools they can use and are expected to use. After a lesson on inserting a vowel into every syllable, it is perfectly reasonable to expect writers to apply that convention in their writing. After a lesson on rereading to check for sentence fragments, it is reasonable to expect writers to reread for the same purpose. As we tiptoe, we can still have high expectations for our students' development and growth.

> ❚❚ The last thing you want is for your children to settle for 'The dog bit at me,' instead of writing 'the dog snarled at me,' because of a concern for correctness. ❚❚
> —*Lucy Calkins and Natalie Louis*

❝ Rereading is the glue that connects the stages of writing. Writers continually reread what they've written, and this rereading changes at each stage of the craft cycle. **❞**

—*Ralph Fletcher*

Rereading Power

- What do I see?

- Is the writing neat enough for someone else to read?

- Do my picture and my words make good use of space on the page?

- Does my punctuation add to the message?

- How is the spelling?

- What words should I revisit?

- Have I used what I know about strong openers and commas to draw in my reader?

Rereading: Strategic Tool for Meaning, Mechanics, and Conventions

- Rereading during *drafting* helps our ideas flow and helps us regain momentum with the message we are crafting.

- Rereading during *revision* helps us wonder about craft elements such as word choice, interesting leads, voice, volume, and focus of information. It is also a time when we can wonder if our punctuation is used in ways that help the reader, add clarity to our thinking or make the writing more interesting.

- Rereading during editing for an audience takes on an entirely different dimension. This is the time when we slow down and really look at the visual dimensions of what we have created.

Rereading: Focused Edits

When students reread to edit for conventions and mechanics, we believe it is most effective for them to engage in focused edits. In a focused edit, the writer reads with a focus on a single purpose. For example, the writer might reread once to check for end punctuation, reread to check for sentence fragments, and then reread a third time, to check for a vowel in each syllable. Each editing point gets its own rereading. Focused edits with a single purpose for each rereading help writers keep a clear focus on the editing purpose.

First focused edit: Reread for capital letters.

Second focused edit: Reread *through a new lens* to reread for end punctuation.

When writers reread for all editing elements at the same time, they can feel overwhelmed and overlook areas where they are capable of using the convention correctly.

❝ Writers take their reading very seriously. When they read, they discover topics for their own writing. They become interested in new genre and formats. They study authors' techniques to learn how to improve their own writing. ❞
—*Shelley Harwayne*

Focus on Reading and Writing as Reciprocal Processes

Reading and writing are reciprocal language processes. As writers create text, they are constantly rereading their work and applying all they know about how print works. When writers read, they are seeing models of language, spacing, conventional spelling, and punctuation that will inform their work as writers (Calkins, 2003). Reading and writing are powerful partners, each extending and transforming the network of literacy understandings being constructed within our students. Research suggests that in classrooms where children write about their reading, embrace mentor texts as writing tutors, and consider writing a natural link to reading, academic achievement is lifted (Taylor, Pearson, Peterson, and Rodriguez, 2002; Graves, 1994). The key is to make the reciprocal relationship between reading and writing transparent to our students as we immerse them in intensive and extensive experiences with print.

Highlight Mechanics and Conventions in Mentor Texts

We have become accustomed to turning to wonderful mentor texts to provide exposure to literary language, form, and craft. It is helpful to consider that children's literature is also one of

When students turn to trusted mentor books as guides to sentence structure, punctuation, and audience, writing is elevated!

our most powerful tools for celebrating and noticing the interesting ways in which writers use spacing, punctuation, capitalization, and grammar. Encouraging students to reread and look closely at a familiar text helps them attend to the fine points, noticing the frequency of end punctuation marks, spacing or purposes for capital letters. Presenting mechanics within literature provides a tapestry of opportunity in which to explore mechanics while helping writers understand that all writers think about spacing, grammar, punctuation, spelling, and so on.

"Scavenger Hunts" through mentor books heighten student awareness of unique uses of punctuation, stimulating the use of punctuation as a support to meaning.

Modeling: The Heart of Our Work

We believe it is critical to do a great deal of modeled writing as the students observe and listen to us think out loud about conventions and mechanics and how they are woven into our messages. We *show* writers how we use punctuation and grammar to make our thinking accessible to a reader. We *show* how to turn to a mentor text for stimulating ideas with commas or how to engage in multiple rereads for editing. Students should have the chance, every day, to observe the creation of quality writing that has artistic punctuation, jaw-dropping phrasing and sets a model that they can attempt to emulate. Just as read-alouds model beautiful language and reading fluency, modeled writing sets a standard for the creation of beautifully constructed writing. The essence lies in *showing*, rather than *telling*, writers what to do.

Crack open the writing process by creating text in front of your students.

Think out loud; let them hear you consider options and make choices.

Show *how* conventions and mechanics fit into our thinking to support meaning.

These explicit demonstrations of writing are central to the work we do as writing coaches. We show intentionality when we model interesting openings, such as insertion of onomatopoeia with an exclamation point or an adverb phrase followed by a comma. We carefully plan and then demonstrate how to create descriptive phrases in a list, how to insert an interrupter into a sentence or how to be reflective about the grammar we utilize in our written work. Through careful modeling, we are clarifying our students' vision of quality writing and raising the standard for quality output.

> **Never ask students to do something they haven't watched you do first.**

Modeled writing, like the picture on the front of a jigsaw puzzle box, sets the stage and helps writers establish a vision of possibility for their work as writers. It is a forum for sharing a broad range of genres, interesting sentence formations, sizzling interjections, and mood-altering phrasing. It is the springboard from which quality student writing evolves. Like read-alouds, modeled writing should be crafted by you as an expert, showing the best of what can be. This is when we show,

rather than tell, what great writing looks like and sounds like. This is *not* a time to write like a child, but rather a time to open the door into the world of wonderful possibility that awaits as writers gain control over their craft. Write at the top of your own game. Pull out all the stops with word choice, phrasing, and interesting punctuation. You will be amazed at how quickly elements of your quality work will begin to appear in the writing of your students.

Think Out Loud During Modeled Writing

The think-alouds we provide during modeled writing make the inner workings of the writing process transparent. If we allow our talk to flow around the creation of printed text, children can listen in as we make decisions about word choice, spelling, punctuation, and grammar. Let them ride with you on your writing journey as you construct and deconstruct your thinking. Talk about what you hope to say, let them hear you think as you make choices, celebrate in front of your students when you think of a fascinating way to use punctuation to power-up your writing. There is no more powerful lesson for your students than watching as you think out loud about phrasing or word choice, pausing midstream to reread and see how everything is coming together, and then return to drafting again.

Important Note: Save your modeled writings! Students like to refer back to them, and you can reuse them for think-alouds on editing, proofreading, and revising.

During a modeled write, the focus is on cracking open the writing process so the internal thinking of an experienced writer becomes transparent to the students.

Think-alouds during modeled writing open the door to the wonders that occur as we think, write, reread, then write again. Think-alouds show learners how we massage messages, selecting the words and the conventions that make our ideas come alive on paper.

Model Rereading and Marking Up a Text

As we model drafting, revising, and editing, we need to help students understand that these essential processes can be messy work. Fourth and fifth graders need to observe us changing our mind, crossing out words or even entire lines. They need to see how we might read a line, stand back, and say something like:

> I just wrote, "The dog barked." That is okay, but it sure isn't very interesting. I am going to scratch that out and write this sentence another way. This is a good time to use what I know about <u>sentence openers and commas</u> to make the sentence sparkle. What do you think of, "With a low rumble from deep in his chest, the dog's bark erupted into a storm of moving fur."

A rewrite like this isn't tidy, but is it good for writers? You bet! Show your students how to actively wrestle with the creation of clear, sparkling messages that are empowered by punctuation

Writing is not necessarily neat and tidy. Let writers see how rereading and marking up a text can improve the quality of the writing.

and strong visual images. Show them how to scratch out and get a bit messy as they draft. Help them understand that this is what writers do during drafting, revising, and again during editing, when they are looking to first draw a reader into the moment, then fine-tune spelling, spacing, punctuation, and so forth. A well-marked-up page often suggests that the writer/editor is thinking deeply.

Joys of Fluent Writing

Writing in fourth and fifth grades is exciting. Students at this age have a sense of fluency and purpose as they pick up their writing tools. They have control over a range of text forms such as personal narrative, procedural texts, descriptive reports, and personal letters. At this stage of writing development, we can expect that most will show variation in sentence beginnings and have a sense of organization and purpose for their work. What we must focus on now is lifting sentence structure, incorporating vocabulary with strength, and utilizing mechanics and conventions to craft writing that sizzles with possibility.

> ### Head Lice
> I have this teacher She is really nice. But some time I think she has head lice. She itches all day. And the last time for head lice check she got sent home from school. I want tell you more but it is Not cool. The day she came back she had no hair and her head was bear. I think to my self how did she get the lice. I kept on thinking untell I new that I was not nice because I'm the one who gave her the lice.
>
> By: Samantha

Fourth and fifth graders are ready to launch into higher levels of craft, using punctuation as a deliberate tool in elevating sentence complexity and clarity. They are ready to shift text forms to suit their audience and purpose. They are ready to push themselves to more sophisticated vocabulary use, sentence structure, and paragraphing (Department of Education, Western

Some hallmarks of writers in 4th and 5th grade

- Considers purpose and audience
- Establishes time, place and situation
- Uses a variety of sentence patterns
- Selects vocabulary to match purpose and for precision
- Groups sentences into paragraphs
- Can replicate elements of craft from mentor texts in their own writing
- Can identify parts of speech and their functions in reading and in their own writing
- Uses transition words and connectors
- Uses appropriate subject/verb agreement
- Uses appropriate noun/pronoun agreement
- Maintains appropriate tense throughout
- Uses a variety of end punctuations
- Uses punctuation to enhance meaning and to control flow of sentences

Australia, 2006). These writers are ready to master the mechanics at a high level of proficiency that will infuse conventions into their thinking during drafting as well as while editing.

The Importance of Approximation

While fourth and fifth graders have an arsenal of sound/symbol relationships and sight words that facilitate their work as writers, they still need to be encouraged to approximate spelling during drafting. Consciously applied approximations help writers stay focused on meaning and rich word choices while they craft ideas. Students learn that when they use approximations, they can return to address spelling during editing. When students utilize these draft-level spelling approximations, they should employ visual and meaning-based strategies. They ask themselves if a word looks right, if it is used in the correct context, if it utilizes spelling patterns, and so on. Drafts should show evidence of rule-based thinking about spelling patterns and a conscious integration of knowledge about root words and units of meaning.

Strategic approximations free writers to "keep writing" and ensure that they will reach for the richest, most exciting word choices rather than settle for

Some approximation demonstrations you might want to consider for this age group include:

- Develop a sense of spelling consciousness… the awareness of spellings that cues you to notice that a word doesn't quite look right.

- Applying multiple strategies: If this doesn't look right, then I will try ___.

- Write your best guess for the word, then draw a line under the word or write an "sp" to remind yourself to check the spelling of the word once you have completed the draft.

- Try several spellings for a word. Use a separate sheet of paper or the margin of your draft to try a word several different ways.

- Use words you know to help you spell other words.

- Break words into syllables, checking for vowels in each syllable.

- Use what you know about letter patterns, such as silent letters, double letters, and so on.

- Consider root words and prefix and suffix patterns.

- Use context to distinguish homophones and homographs.

- After drafting, turn to dictionaries and other resources, such as thesauruses, portable word walls, and editing checklists.

words they can spell correctly. This sense of reaching for greatness is critical if we are to create resourceful and independent writers who realize that waiting in line for teacher-provided spelling may cause them to lose track of their thought and create an unnecessary dependency. But again, we must model… To validate the use of approximation, we must demonstrate strategies to approximate spelling.

Modeling Word Construction

While modeling word construction, we model how to write a little "sp" above the word or underline a word when we do not feel confident about its spelling to indicate the word needs checking. We think out loud about common spelling patterns when writing a word like *transition*. In a word like this, we would expect to see /sion/ or /tion/. Which pattern might this word utilize? Which spelling looks right? We even model breaking a word into syllables and remembering that each syllable needs at least one vowel:

> Writers, you are not only creating interesting writing that I am itching to read, you are getting better and better at breaking words into syllables to help yourselves spell. That is a very helpful strategy that I use while I am drafting and again when I am editing. Let's look together at this writing that I did a few days ago. I am going to think about the syllables in my words and check that I have at least one vowel for each syllable. I wrote, "It was a regular Saturday afternoon…" As I think about syllables, I don't need to check every word. Some words are very short, some I am sure I spelled correctly. I am going to check *regular* and *afternoon*. *Reg/u/lar*. I hear three syllables. I will underline the vowels to check that I have a vowel in each syllable. Now, I will check *afternoon*. Think together. How many syllables in *afternoon*?

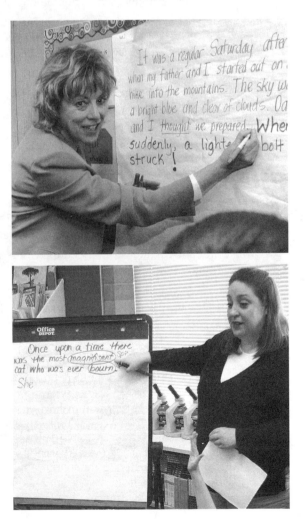

> Spelling isn't just about correctness. It is also about developing a set of spelling strategies that enable a writer to problem-solve during drafting, notice when words are not spelled correctly during editing, and establish a sense of spelling consciousness. A strategic speller applies spelling strategies throughout the writing process, crafting text with fluency and editing with an eye for convention.

Thinking About Audience

> **"** {With a focus on a reader} ...the writer will have to take an idea and shape it with genre, form, sound, and the conventions of the language system all working together to produce a piece that has the desired impact on readers.**"**
>
> —*Katie Wood Ray*
> *and Lisa Cleaveland*

Fourth- and fifth-grade writers are approaching conventional writing and have the capability of keeping their audience in mind as they draft, revise, and edit. This sense of audience adds strength to written text as writers must constantly reread their work from the perspective of the readers. The writers must wonder if readers will understand the messages, be able to read the spelling, and understand pause points and the flow of ideas. Although we can be our own audience for our writing, writers must internally shift from writing for personal expression to writing with their readers in mind. When there is an authentic audience for their work, authors have strong and viable purposes for looking more closely at their work and expecting more from the print they create.

To build a sense of audience, we believe it is important to provide authentic reasons for students to share their writing. Activities such as partner sharing, author's chair, end-of-workshop sharing circles,

Ideas for Creating Authentic Audience

- Write notes to each other and the teacher.
- Write letters to parents and ask the parents to write back.
- Write and mail letters to request travel brochures or information on particular states.
- Involve students in drafting and editing a class newsletter that goes to parents at least once a month.
- Create partnerships with another class so writers can read their writing to another authentic audience.
- Publish class books and individual books.
- Create student-made or -designed posters of processes and procedures for writing or classroom management.
- Post writing on the walls of the classroom that exemplify a specific craft element such as: Interesting Leads, Great Use of Interjections, Two-Word Sentences Mixed in With Longer Sentences, Finding Freedom From Fragments, Writing Transformed by Rereading.
- Make student-created bulletin boards with sentence strips highlighting great moments in literature.

> **Famous Authors Grab Readers' Attention With Sentence Openers Followed by Comma**

> **Favorite Authors Show Emotion: Interjections, Exclamations, and Caps for Emphasis**

> **Fascinating Commas Found in Favorite Books**

- Provide "From the Desk of _____" pads and have students write notes for authentic purposes. (See Tools section page 161.)
- Write Get Well cards to fellow students and school personnel.
- Create interactive posters comparing the number of commas in *Amos and Boris* and *Shrek*, both by William Steig. Include sentence strips with favorite examples of sentences with interesting use of commas.

From the Desk of

_____

Fourth and fifth graders love to write notes. Why not legalize note writing with "From the Desk of _____" forms. Students can write reminders to themselves, their friends, the teacher, or parents.

and publishing all help. But we can go further. When writers have a clear understanding that their work will be public, mechanics and conventions become important in a personal way. Unfortunately, the teacher as audience has limited appeal. Editing and conventions utilized just to please the teacher quickly become tedious and boring.

Authentic audience and authentic purposes work hand in hand to provide motivation and a rationale for why conventions and mechanics are important. This is the time when we reread for "correctness" and for lifting the visual aspects of our message to the highest possible levels.

Authentic audiences build intrinsic motivation for improving the quality of mechanics and conventions.

"Students can hear all we have to say about punctuation, but, if there are no real-life connections, little will stick."
—Janet Angelillo

The Environment

The environment we create for writing is important. A rich environment for writing should have areas for:

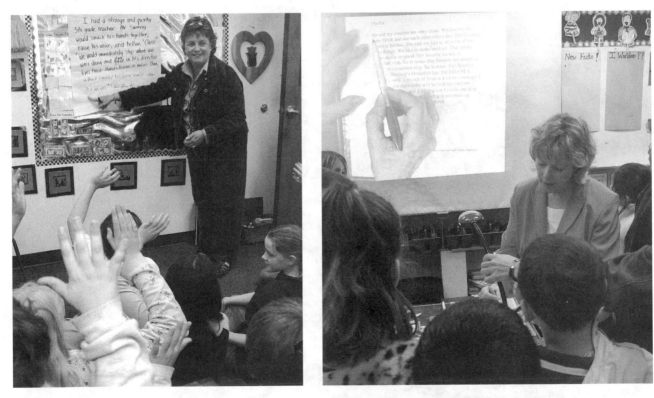

Modeled writing and teacher think-aloud

Guided practice at an overhead or document camera

Partner editing

Editing conferences and coaching for individuals

The walls should make strong statements about the learning in the classroom. Modeled writing, word walls, editing checklists, and posters showing studies of conventions should be clearly visible. Bulletin boards should celebrate craft elements and strategies in action. Mentor books should be clearly displayed with labeling that points out the conventions and mechanics that are particularly evident in each selection.

As you explore mentor books, work with students to create posters of terrific model sentences and post them in a visible place.

"Scavenger Hunts" for interesting openers followed by commas, or punctuation used in interesting ways heighten students' awareness of conventions. The results of Scavenger Hunts can be displayed on bulletin boards as resources for writers.

Interactive posters built collaboratively with students make strong statements about the importance of conventions and mechanics in published literature and in our own work as writers.

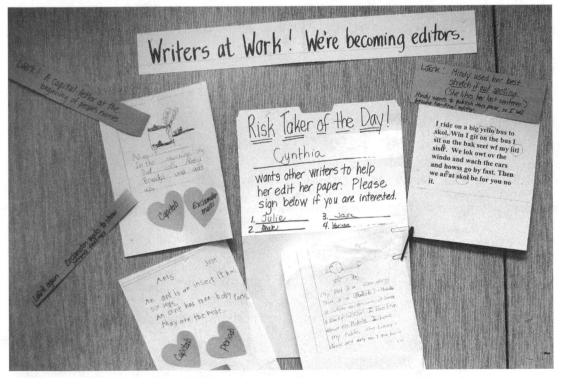

The walls should tell a story of writers and the tools they use to empower their craft. When student work is posted, it should be for a clear purpose that heightens awareness of conventions or elevates craft. Notice how this display invites editors to offer team support to a writer as she edits her work. This sets a model for collaborative thinking and highlights the importance of careful editing.

Editing Checklist — Reread
Check over your writing.
Make your writing reable.

☐ Use capitals → at the beginning of sentences My dog runs fast.
people's names Joseph Cecelia Mrs. Hogan

☑ Use my best spelling. YES!!
☑ Mark words that don't look right. YES!!!
☑ NEVER, NEVER, NEVER EVER stop writing to ask how to spell a word.
Keep those ideas flowing!!!

☑ Reread my writing and check for 1 thing at a time.

Editing checklists should emphasize your students' current phase of development and change over time to reflect new learning. Involve students in the development of editing checklists so they have a voice in the tools that support their writing.

Words to Contrast
Although	But
Differ	Even though
However	In contrast
Instead	Nevertheless
On the contrary	Unlike
While	Yet

These words signal the reader that your two ideas are different.

With a grin of sheer delight, I lifed the warm, gooey cookie to my lips. Mmmm Good!

Pop! Sizzle! Zing! The heated kernels vibrated madly as they prepared to explode. Boom! Like a bomb, it goes kaboom.

Modeled writing samples should be available for students to revisit over time. These can become a resource for interesting language patterns, unique punctuation, and a celebration of conventions.

Model the Use of Classroom Tools

When classroom walls reflect a rich tapestry of writing forms, tools, and supports, a strong message is sent to students, parents, colleagues, and the community that this is a classroom where writing and mechanics are celebrated and savored. It is important to remember, however, that rich visuals provide invitations, but real use will occur only with explicit and careful modeling of the tools in action.

We believe that we must model the use of word walls, charts, and environmental print so our students understand that as writers, we select our tools carefully. Like a carpenter, we must select the tools that match our purposes and know when to use each one. *During prewriting*, we may turn to a mentor text for guidance on using commas in interesting ways or examine eye-catching punctuation in opening sentences. Our mentor texts may include modeled writing done by the teacher, the work of a peer, or a favorite picture book, such as *Owl Moon* by Jane Yolen.

During drafting, we generally minimize the use of tools, using portable word walls and class word walls only if we are sure we can find a word so quickly it won't interrupt our message.

> **Visuals are only helpful if students actively use them.**

Then, during editing for an audience, we shift our stance and emphasize tools that will help us reach higher in our use of conventions and mechanics. This is the time when editing checklists, word walls, and other resources empower our thinking and help us and our writing to grow. Editing is also a time when we can view classmates as powerful resources and enter into editing partnerships.

When you demonstrate and think aloud about your options for using tools while you are modeling writing, students develop a deeper understanding of how tools empower and lift writing. Talk to writers about why you are or are not electing to turn to a resource or use a tool. Be deliberate as you consider whether a tool will help you or distract you from your message. Let students hear you consider the use of a tool such as a class word wall, then decide to wait until editing. Let them see you walk to a tool such as a homophone chart while editing, then use the tool to consider a word choice. Tools are helpful resources if writers take an active stance in their use.

Class Lists of Conventions and Mechanics

Class editing lists that grow with each cycle in this resource provide a cumulative record of your cycles. This keeps writers focused on what they have learned. This cumulative record of lessons is a powerful visual reminder to writers of their evolving control over print. With each cycle, writers will notice that they are reminded to pause, review the class poster, and then add a new understanding. Because this list is displayed in a clearly visible place, writers can use it as a tool to assist their planning before drafting, as a reference while writing or to support their thinking while editing.

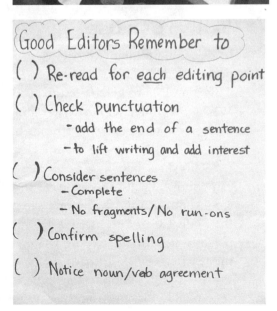

Good Editors Remember to
( ) Re-read for e*ach* editing point
( ) Check punctuation
    - add the end of a sentence
    - to lift writing and add interest
( ) Consider sentences
    - Complete
    - No fragments / No run-ons
( ) Confirm spelling
( ) Notice noun/verb agreement

Writing Folders and Personal Tools to Support Editors

Editors need personal tools, such as a well-organized writing folder to store their work and keep personal tools readily at hand. These personal tools might include topic lists, writers' notebooks, portable word walls, editing checklists, small dictionaries, and lists of skills that writers will be accountable for using in their completed pieces. Some classrooms even find that it is helpful to use the main writing folder for "pieces in progress" and then warehouse finished pieces in a separate folder.

When writers have a well-organized writing folder, writing and personal tools are easily accessible.

Writing folders should have a place where learners can record skills or conventions they can use as writers. Once items are on their personal list, writers know they are accountable for applying these skills every time they edit. See Tools section, page 169 for a template.

Skills I Can Use

In designing folders, we believe it is very helpful to keep a sheet of paper titled "Skills I Can Use" attached to one side of the folder. This is a place to celebrate the accomplishments of each student. When we confer with a writer and observe that the student has correctly applied a convention or mechanic, we celebrate by writing the skill on the Skills I Can Use page and dating it.

This sheet becomes a record of the skills each individual writer can control. Each time we have an editing conference and work on a convention, a mechanic or a spelling strategy, we add the skill to the Skills I Can Use list and date the entry. This list is an ongoing, personal reminder—for the writer, the writer's editing partner, and the teacher—of skills that have been mastered by each individual. Once a skill is added to their lists, students take pride in their learning and know they are now accountable for applying the skill in every piece of writing that will have an audience.

Editing Checklists

The goal of editing checklists is to teach students to take responsibility to reread and be their own first editors. The checklist, in combination with Skills I Can Use pages and class editing posters, scaffolds learners for success. Checklists are tools that support students' use of known skills. They do not provide instruction.

> It is important to remember that editing checklists do not "teach;" they simply remind students to use the processes that you have modeled.

> Remember focused edits: Simultaneous rereading for every element on a checklist can be too great of a challenge and result in less effective editing. Each item on an editing checklist should get its own focused edit. If there are four items on the checklist, writers will reread at least four times.

Just as we differentiate in other areas of the curriculum, personal editing checklists can be modified to scaffold and support learners across the range of writing experiences in your classroom. We encourage you to explore the checklists in the Assessment section of this resource, pages 165–166. While these examples may offer matches to some of your students, consider creating your own editing checklists that match precisely with the *Mastering the Mechanics* cycles you have selected for instruction.

Checklists for Partner Editing

Once writers review their work on their own, they are ready to engage in partner edits. During partner editing, writers collaboratively use editing checklists and their shared sense of language and convention to lift a piece to a level that an individual writer may not have reached alone.

> We like to encourage the following steps, modeled after Day 2 of our editing cycles, for "Partner Editing for an Audience."
>
> 1. The author reads his or her piece to a partner or partners.
> 2. The partners offer a compliment about the message.
> 3. The partner and the author together begin a series of focused edits using an editing checklist.
> 4. The team then decides whether to invite in another editor for a last round of edits or that the piece is ready for a teacher editing conference.

Creating Checklists With Your Students

When students are involved in creating editing checklists, they must reflect on what they know about conventions and mechanics, then design tools that will help them to be accountable for what they know. We believe strongly in having students work with us in whole-class and small-group settings to design editing checklists that match phases of development or apply to a specific kind of writing. Writers gain a profound sense of ownership and empowerment when they develop their own editing checklists.

The Teaching/Assessing Loop

Assessment is our essential guide to quality instruction. As we observe writers during drafting, meet with them in small groups or confer with individuals, we are constantly assessing to determine what they do and do not know. Our assessments are the best possible guides to instruction. The data we gather through thoughtful, sensitive assessment helps us choose the next skills our students need and also helps us determine whether our students are fully grasping the material we're teaching.

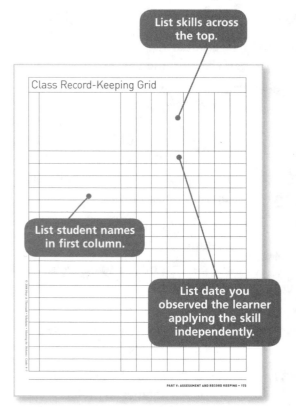

List skills across the top.

Class Record-Keeping Grid

List student names in first column.

List date you observed the learner applying the skill independently.

PART V: ASSESSMENT AND RECORD KEEPING • 173

Helpful tip: Photocopy the Class Record-Keeping Grid after you have entered student names in the first column and you will be ready to gather data on a wide variety of skills without having to write student names each time.

Selecting Editing Skills for Instruction

To determine which conventions and mechanics are expected at a particular grade level, look first at your state standards. We suggest that you consider highlighting these standards on a photocopy of the skills continuum located on pages 31–36. If you are working with a mandated language arts resource, you might identify the skills for spelling, punctuation, grammar, and so on in the program, then highlight those on the grid as well. (We like to add program-driven goals in a second color so we can see where they deviate from state standards.) Now, as you look at the skills grid, you have a unified picture that shows state standards and program requirements in a single, easy-to-follow format that will round out your editing work with fourth- and fifth-grade writers. Then you can assess the skills your students are already implementing in their writing.

Assess the Skills Your Students Can Use

We feel it is critical to collect unedited writing samples and use the class record-keeping grids provided in the Assessment section, pages 173–176. It takes only minutes to list student names in the first column and jot target conventions and mechanics across the top of the other columns. With a stack of writing samples in hand, you are ready to start placing checkmarks for writers whose work demonstrates punctuation in dialogue, subject-verb agreement, and so on.

Once you have a profile of your students and their needs, you are ready to select a cycle and "master the mechanics!"

In the "How An Octopus…" example, our assessment review shows that this writer is using some transition words to link ideas (*first*, *then*). The sentences are complete. One sentence, "When an animal tries to attack her…" uses a strong opening with a comma to draw in the reader. This writer/editor would benefit from some work on paragraphs and headings, which are conventions of organization that make informational text more manageable for a reader. So to fill out the chart, we could place a tally or date observed under transition words, openers with a comma, and complete sentences. Since this is only one example, we would wait to collect more evidence of these skills before assuming that the writer has truly mastered the learning.

In any case, assessment leads the way to quality instruction.

With the support of the grid, we quickly expose patterns of strengths and needs for individuals, small groups, and the class as a whole. The grid allows us to identify groups of writers who share similar needs and to easily gather small groups for explicit instruction or to confer with individual writers. We find this assessment tool

> How An Octopus Protects Herself
>
> An octopus has many ways to protect herself. First she can take her eight legs and wrap them around other animals. She can use the suction cups on her legs to grip things. When an animal tries to attack her, she can make her body squish together so she can hide out in little places. That was a surprise to me! An octopus can squirt ink into the water and blind the attacker for a little bit of time. Then she swims off. Pretty cool. ways to protect herself.
>
> by Stephanie J.

Notice Teresa using the clipboard and grid during writing conferences and when moving around the room to assist writers.

so helpful that we keep it on a clipboard while circulating during writer's workshop and as a reference during writing conferences.

Notice Oral Language Patterns

Grammar in student writing is tightly linked to oral language. With this in mind, we challenge ourselves to *listen* carefully and try to notice which students need support with noun/verb agreement, verb tenses, or use of pronouns in oral speech. You may hear your students using oral patterns such as, "My mom, she went to the store." "Me and Bobby raced on our skateboards." "I seen a dog trying to get in the school." Record your observations and compare the patterns you notice in oral language with those in your students' writing. This provides a balanced assessment of oral and written language use that can help you make critical decisions about which cycles to select. If you have only a small group of students for whom grammatical structures are an issue, you may elect to differentiate by engaging a small group in a cycle directly targeted to its needs. If many of your students are challenged by the same grammatical structure, the grammar cycles on this topic may be the perfect choice for the entire class. Again, assessment leads the way to quality instruction.

Supporting and Respecting

We must always respect home language and community culture, yet we have a responsibility to help learners understand and apply the more formal registers of English that are seen in published books and expected of proficient writers. While we would never show disrespect to language patterns that are native to the children, it may be helpful to explain to students that language shifts to match the audience. For example, we speak to the principal or a police officer differently than we do to our friends on the playground. There are certain formal registers of language that we are expected to use as writers that aren't always expected when we talk to our friends or relax in our homes.

To support conventional grammar use, we can highlight conventional grammar in our favorite books, think aloud about grammar while crafting sentences during modeled writing, or respond with elaborated language when students use nonstandard structures. The trick to elaborating and extending language use is to mirror the learner's message using correct form in your response. There is no reprimand for incorrect usage, you simply mirror what the student has said by restating it in conventional English.

A few examples:

If a student says:	You might reply:
I seen a dog trying to get in the school.	You *saw* a dog trying to get in? Would you like to notify the custodian?
Me and my dad went fishing.	*My dad and I* used to go fishing, too. Did you have a wonderful time?
My sister, she fell and broke her arm.	*Your sister fell* and broke her arm! How awful. How is she doing?
We don't got no paper towels.	We don't *have any* paper towels? Would you like to write a note to the custodian so he knows?

Editing Conferences: Adding the Chocolate Swirls

Assuming that you have already held a revision conference with the writer, an editing conference is at least the second time when you and the writer can think together about a piece of writing. The first time, the emphasis was on meaning, which may have included the use of interesting punctuation to lift the writing. This time the focus of the conference is editing.

During this conference, select one or two skills to address with the student. Never teach more than one or two things at a time. Writers are not likely to retain more information. We like to keep sticky notes in hand during editing conferences as we believe that when writers make their own corrections and retain control of the pencil, they are more likely to remember and reuse what they have learned. By jotting suggested edits on sticky notes, writers retain control of the pen and understand that they have a responsibility to edit their own work. During an editing conference, the writer is responsible for his or her actions. This is not about teacher corrections. It is about guiding them as they move forward in their use of conventions and mechanics.

With this in mind, an editing conference might sound something like the following:

> Alexa, you must be so pleased you have decided to publish your piece on skateboarding. As a reader, I could totally visualize the tension of entering a half-pipe and the enormous energy you expend as you try to get air for a spin. Your verbs were very powerful and made a big difference in my ability to visualize the action.
>
> As we begin editing, please tell me what you and your editing partner have already discovered and worked on in your writing. Be sure to point out any changes or additions you and your editing partner were able to make.
>
> I see that you are really prepared for this editing conference. You have underlined six words that you want to look at for spelling, have used a sticky note to jot your question on the grammar in this last sentence, and brought the skateboarding book to use as a reference. These are terrific strategies that are important to top-notch editing. I have some sticky notes we can use to record suggestions for editing, then you can return to your desk and enter any changes required in the piece.

Steps for Editors When Writing for an Audience

We teach writers that if they are going to have an audience for their writing, they need to follow these last steps as editors:

1. Use the editing checklist to do a focused edit for each item on the list.

2. Find an editing partner. Read the writing together and think about making it the best it can be.

3. Sign up for an editing conference with the teacher.

Editing conferences anchor learning with personal attention and support.

A Note About the Yearlong Planner

The Yearlong Planner featured on the gatefold (the inside front cover) of this book is a tool to help you map your curriculum for mechanics and conventions for the year. As you can see, this planner provides week-by-week suggestions for three content cycles followed by a Pulling It All Together cycle to solidify the learning with authentic, interactive purpose. During a Pulling It All Together Cycle, no new skills are added. This is a time for learners to apply their learning from the previous Cycles in authentic contexts. With this plan as your guide, students will have four weeks of instruction and opportunities to transfer skills to long-term memory.

Please note on page 163 there is a blank version of the Yearlong Planner. With this planner, you can use your own assessments along with your state standards to build a personalized curriculum map.

Important Note: This sample planner does not contain all of the lessons in this resource. We built a range of lessons to support your responses to the needs of your students. There are many paths through this resource. You may elect to use all of the planner or portions of it, or you can select lessons based entirely upon the needs of your learners. The choices and the path you select are up to you.

On Your Way!

The lesson cycles that are the centerpiece of this resource are meant to celebrate writers and their ever-growing control over craft and form. As you enter these cycles, we challenge you to recast conventions and mechanics as tools for enhancing meaning and to have a joyous journey as you "master the mechanics."

PART II

Skills Continuum

The skills continuum profiles the spectrum of development in mechanics and conventions that might be expected from learners in the elementary grades. For ease of use, it is divided into sections that match the organizational structure of the lessons.

Each convention listed on the continuum is supported by an explanation that often includes an example for clarity. To the right of each listed convention is a designation of grade level(s) at which writers should be exposed to and learn to implement the convention. When a convention is supported by a lesson in this resource, the page number on which the lesson appears is also listed.

You may find it helpful to photocopy the continuum and keep a copy on a clipboard. This way the continuum can serve as"

- a quick reference when planning your own mini-lessons or cycles of support for conventions

- a source of support when conferring with students during writing conferences

- a place to keep track of focus lessons on a convention that you provide

Overall, the continuum should offer a broad-based view of your students' writing development across the range of mechanics, conventions, and processes that good editors use, and it should empower your thinking as you differentiate instruction for the range of learners you serve.

Sections of the Continuum:

Processes Editors Use

Capitalization

Punctuation

Grammar

Spacing

Spelling

Page where lesson appears in this book	Conventions & Mechanics	Explanation	K	1	2	3	4	5
	PROCESSES EDITORS USE							
	Putting your name on the paper	Writers should habitualize writing their names on papers before creating text or drawings.	•	•				
	Counting the words in a message	Before writing, young writers count the words in their message to match speech to print.	•	•				
	Reread and touch each word	Writers touch each word to check for omissions.	•	•	•			
38	**Reread to focus on message**	Meaning is always our first emphasis when creating text. Writers must reread to confirm or revise for meaning before focusing on surface conventions.	•	•	•	•	•	•
	Reread to edit for conventions	Once meaning is clear, writers reread to check for surface structures and grammar that give our writing uniformity.	•	•	•	•	•	•
40	**Focused edit: reread for each editing point**	Rereading helps writers check for surface structures and grammar. The piece is read once for each editing point.	•	•	•	•	•	•
40	**Using an editing checklist**	Checklists matched to developmental levels of writers are used to guide personal and partner edits.	•	•	•	•	•	•
42	**Use copyediting symbols to support editing**	Authors and editing partners use standardized copyediting symbols to identify and support their editorial work.				•	•	•
	Edit with a partner	When partners work together to proofread, they elevate each other's thinking about text.	•	•	•	•	•	•
	Celebrate and self-reflect	To grow, writers must take time to reflect on their own growth as communicators of meaning.	•	•	•	•	•	•
	CAPITALIZATION							
	Capitalize the pronoun "I"	I am going to Anna's house.	•	•	•	•	•	•
	Use mostly lowercase letters	Capital letters need to be used for specific purposes.	•	•				
	Capitalize the beginning of sentences	Capitalize the first word in each sentence.	•	•	•	•	•	•
46	**Capitalize proper nouns: names and places**	My sister, Anna, is taking dance lessons in Seattle. She hopes to perform at the Keller Auditorium.	•	•	•	•	•	•
	Capitalize a title before a name	Mrs. Jones works in the office of Judge Jacobs	•	•	•	•	•	•
	Capitalize proper adjectives	Proper adjectives are formed from a noun used as an adjective: American figure skaters; French bread.				•	•	•
	Capitalize days of the week	Monday, Tuesday	•	•	•	•	•	•
50	**Capitalize titles**	*Where the Wild Things Are, My Swimming Party*	•	•	•	•	•	•
48	**Capitalize for emphasis**	HOORAY!		•	•	•	•	•
50	**Capitalize AM and PM**	Abbreviations for morning and afternoon need to be capitalized when they are written without a period.			•	•	•	•
50	**Capitalize abbreviations for state names (OR, CA, NY)**	Names of states are abbreviated with two capital letters.			•	•	•	•

Page	Skill	Description						
	Common nouns can become proper nouns	A common noun, used as a name of a person, is capitalized when there is no possessive or article preceding it. Grandma and Mom went shopping. Grandma and my mom went shopping.			•	•	•	•

PUNCTUATION

Page	Skill	Description						
54	**Periods: end of sentence**	Declarative sentences need a period at the end.	•	•	•	•	•	•
	Period with abbreviation	Mr. Jones; a.m. or p.m.				•	•	•
54	**Exclamation points: exclamatory sentences and interjections**	An exclamation point is used for emphasis. Examples: Drip! Drop! I can't believe it is still raining!	•	•	•	•	•	•
54	**Question marks: interrogative sentences**	Question marks are placed at the end of sentences that inquire.	•	•	•	•	•	•
64	**Commas: use in a series**	I need to buy shoes, socks, an umbrella and a jacket.		•	•	•	•	•
	Comma to separate day of the month and year	December 28, 2008		•	•	•	•	•
	Comma to separate city and state	Portland, Oregon		•	•	•	•	•
74	**Comma following a transition word at the beginning of sentences**	Finally, our long-awaited order arrived.		•	•	•	•	•
66	**Comma precedes a connecting word (coordinating conjunction) when combining two short sentences**	Anna has my library book, and Devon has my lunch. (Examples of connecting words: so, or, but, and)		•	•	•	•	•
	Comma with direct address	Anna, grab your coat!			•	•	•	•
	Commas in a letter	Place a comma after the greeting and the closing.		•	•	•	•	•
72	**Comma surrounds an appositive**	Anna, the amazing runner, won the medal.			•	•	•	•
68	**Comma: After introductory phrase or clause**	When they heard the final bell, the children headed for the bus.			•	•	•	•
70	**Comma to set off closer**	The children tiptoed down the hall, wondering what would happen next.					•	•
56	**Punctuation in dialogue**	"Hurry up!" cried Anna. "Can you help me find my keys?" her mother asked.	•	•	•	•	•	•
58	**Apostrophe: contractions**	Can't, won't, shouldn't	•	•	•	•	•	•
60	**Apostrophe: Possessives**	Anna's bike is bright yellow.	•	•	•	•	•	•
	Colon in reporting the time	10:30 a.m.			•	•	•	•
	Colon at the beginning of a list	They had a long list of errands, including the following: going to the grocery store, the post office, and the health food store.			•	•	•	•
	Hyphen to join compound descriptions	Heavy-handed dog trainer; father-in-law.				•	•	•
	Hyphen to separate syllables	At the end of a line if there isn't room for the entire word, syllables are separated with a hyphen.				•	•	•
	Underline or italicize a book title	When a book or play title is handwritten, it should be underlined.				•	•	•

Page	Term	Description						
	Ellipses	Use ellipses to indicate a pause in thought, or the omission of words or sentences. Example: I won't go, but. . .				•	•	•

GRAMMAR

Page	Term	Description						
78	Complete sentences	Writers avoid unintentional sentence fragments (The fuzzy puppy) and need to acquire a strong foundation in writing complete, interesting sentences (The fuzzy puppy howled at the moon.).	•	•	•	•	•	•
	Phrase	A phrase is a group of words that takes the place of a specific part of speech. *The house at the end of the street* is a phrase that acts like a noun. The phrase *at the end of the street* is a prepositional phrase that acts like an adjective.			•	•	•	•
	Clause	A clause is a word or group of words ordinarily consisting of a subject and a predicate. A clause usually contains a verb and may or may not be a sentence in its own right. (Example: I didn't know that the cat ran up the tree. *That the cat ran up the tree* is a clause. This clause includes the phrase *up the tree*.)				•	•	•
	Sentence parts: simple subject and simple verb	Writers understand the essential components of a sentence, the who or what does something (subject) and what the subject does (verb). Toddlers scamper. Brian cheered.		•	•	•	•	•
	Control sentence length vs. run-on sentences	Writers use simple, compound, or complex sentences to enrich writing, while avoiding run-ons. Nonstandard: The fuzzy puppy snuggled in my arms and then he ate fast and played and barked and then he. . . Standard: The fuzzy puppy, while snuggling in my arms, fell quickly asleep. Then, he. . .		•	•	•	•	•
74	Using transition words	Transition words are used to organize writing and alert readers to changes in the text. (Finally, our long awaited order arrived.)	•	•	•	•	•	•
	Singular and plural nouns	Writers understand the difference between singular and plural nouns, and can form plurals.	•	•	•	•	•	•
90	Single vs. double subject	Writers avoid the nonstandard double subject (My mom she prefers. . .) and select single subjects for sentences (My mom prefers. . .).	•	•	•	•	•	•
92	Singular subject-verb agreement	A singular noun and pronoun (subject) agrees with its verb in number, case, and person. (Singular: Mary giggles.)	•	•	•	•	•	•
94	Plural subject-verb agreement	Plural nouns and pronouns (subjects) agree with their verbs in number, case, and person. (Plural: The babies wobble.)	•	•	•	•	•	•
84	Verb tenses: present and past	Writers differentiate between present- and past-tense verbs to show *when* an action takes place. (I sit on the edge of my bed. I sat on the edge of my bed.)	•	•	•	•	•	•
84	Verb tense: future	Writers expand their use of verbs to show a future action or state of being. (Mario will be a stellar teacher.)	•	•	•	•	•	•
88	Verb types: action	The most common verb is the action verb that tells what the subject is doing. (Mario swims across the lake.)	•	•	•	•	•	•
88	Verb types: linking	Writers use linking verbs (nonaction verbs) to connect the subject with nouns, pronouns, or adjectives that follow. Linking verbs: *is, are, was, were*. (Margarita is my maternal aunt.)	•	•	•	•	•	•
88	Verb types: main	When a verb is composed of two or more words, the verb at the end of the verb phrase is the main (principal) verb. (Anna is dancing down the hall.)				•	•	•
88	Verb types: helping	Writers use helping (auxiliary) verbs to create verb phrases that consist of the helping verb and the main (principal) verb. (Anna is dancing down the hall.)			•	•	•	•
86	Verb forms: regular	Most verbs are regular. Writers add *ed* to show a past action, or use a helping verb (*has, had, have*).				•	•	•

Page	Skill	Description						
86	**Verb forms: irregular**	Some verbs are irregular. Their past-tense form is not made by adding *ed* or when using helping verbs. Past tense is expressed with a new word (*run, ran*).			•	•	•	•
96	**Pronoun order (person's name and then *I*, not *me*)**	Standard form: My mom and I... My mom, dad, and I... Nonstandard: Me and my mom. Me and my dad and my mom...	•	•	•	•	•	•
98	**Pronouns and their antecedents**	Writers identify the nouns to which pronouns refer. Standard: Niva is an exceptional cook. She whipped up dinner last night. Nonstandard: She is an exceptional cook. She whipped up dinner last night.		•	•	•	•	•
100	**Possessive pronouns**	Possessive pronouns take the place of a noun and show ownership. Most possessive pronouns are written without an apostrophe (*my, our, their*).	•	•	•	•	•	•
102	**Subjective and objective cases of pronouns and nouns**	Nouns remain the same for both subjective and objective cases, whereas pronouns require differentiation between the subjective (I, you, he, she, it, we, you, they) and objective (me, you, him, her, it, us, you, them) cases.				•	•	•
	Double negatives	Only one word should be used to express a negative idea. Frequent errors occur when writers use *not* with *never, no, hardly,* and so on. Standard: We don't have any paper towels. Nonstandard: We don't have no paper towels.				•	•	•
104	**Adjectives to lift descriptions**	Writers include adjectives, words that describe nouns and pronouns, to strengthen text. (The brilliant butterfly zipped past the decrepit barn.)	•	•	•	•	•	•
106	**Adjectives: comparative and superlative forms**	Adjectives can be used to compare two or more people, places, things, or ideas. (Examples: bigger, biggest; more/less helpful; most/least helpful)				•	•	•
	Articles	Articles are adjectives. *The* indicates a specific (definite) article. (Bring me the striped sweater.) *A* and *an* refer to no particular thing. *A* is used before a consonant sound. (Bring me a sweater.) *An* is used before a vowel sound. (Bring me an apple.)		•	•	•	•	•
80	**Adverbs and adverb phrases**	Adverbs modify verbs, adjectives, or other adverbs. Most adverbs tell when, where, how, and to what extent/degree. (Marcos quickly zipped over the goal line.)				•	•	•
108	**Adverbs: comparative and superlative forms**	Adverbs can be used to compare two or more people, places, things, or ideas. (Examples: faster, fastest; more/less carefully; most/least carefully)				•	•	•
	Interjections	Interjections are words or phrases that are used to express a strong emotion and are separated from the rest of the sentence by a comma or an exclamation point. (Wow! This is cool! Wow, this is cool!)	•	•	•	•	•	•
	Prepositions and prepositional phrases	Prepositions are not modifiers; their function is to relate a noun or pronoun to another word in the sentence. A prepositional phrase includes a preposition, the object of the preposition, and any modifiers. (The cat snoozed *under the lawn chair.*)			•	•	•	•
	Conjunctions: coordinating	Conjunctions connect words or groups of words. Coordinating conjunctions connect equal parts: words, phrases, and independent clauses (sentences). (Examples of coordinating conjunctions: for, and, nor, but, or, yet, so)		•	•	•	•	•
	Conjunctions: subordinating	Conjunctions connect words or groups of words. Subordinating conjunctions connect two clauses to make complex sentences. (Examples of subordinating conjunctions: after, because, before, until, when, while)			•	•	•	•

SPACING

Page	Topic	Description	1	2	3	4	5	6
	Word boundaries: keep letters in a word close together	Letters in a word need to be clustered so word boundaries are apparent.	•	•				
	Using entire page	Writers should write from top to bottom, left to right, using return sweep.	•	•				
	Using multiple pages	Writers need to expand their thinking beyond single page writing experiences.	•	•	•	•	•	•
	Margins	Allow appropriate margin, headers and footer spaces.	•	•	•	•	•	•
	Pagination in a multiple-page piece	Page breaks are governed by arrangement around visuals and by available space on a page. Each page in a story should have a page number.	•	•	•	•	•	•
	Spacing of visuals in non-fiction	Visuals carry important messages in nonfiction and can appear in many positions on a page.	•	•	•	•	•	•
	Placement of nonfiction features	Nonfiction features such as the table of contents, captions, headings, index, and glossary have their own conventions for spacing.	•	•	•	•	•	•
	Paragraph breaks	Paragraphs should be arranged on a page so they are clearly set apart from one another.			•	•	•	•
	Spacing in a letter	Spacing for friendly and business letters follows a uniform format for the date, greeting, closing, and signature.		•	•	•	•	•
	Spacing on an envelope	Envelopes have clearly defined spaces for the addressee and the return address.		•	•	•	•	•

SPELLING

Page	Topic	Description	1	2	3	4	5	6
112	**Spelling consciousness**	Students should have a high level of awareness that spelling is important.	•	•	•	•	•	•
	Stretching words	Writers say words slowly to pull them apart auditorily.	•	•	•	•	•	•
	Reread to add more letters	Rereading allows writers opportunities to modify spelling.	•	•	•			
	Big words have more letters than small words	Writers need to expect to use more letters in longer words, as they develop spelling consciousness.	•	•				
	Spelling reference: picture alphabet card	Picture alphabet cards help writers identify sound-symbol relationships.	•	•				
114	**Spelling reference: portable word wall**	Word walls help writers quickly access high-frequency words. Content word walls support spelling of content-specific words.	•	•	•	•	•	•
	Use known words to spell other words.	Spelling by analogy allows students to use known words and word parts to spell other words. If I can write *in*, then I can also write *pin*.	•	•	•	•	•	•
	Noticing syllables: each syllable needs a vowel	Writers need to expect to place at least one vowel in every syllable.	•	•	•	•	•	•
116	**Try different spellings for words**	When faced with an uncertain spelling, writers benefit from trying various spellings in the margin or on a separate sheet of paper.		•	•	•	•	•
118	**Homophones**	Homophones are words that sound the same but have different spellings and meanings (their, there, they're; no, know)		•	•	•	•	•

PART III

Lesson Cycles for Mastering the Mechanics

Rereading for multiple purposes helps writers look closely at meaning and conventions.

Cycles for Understanding the Editing Process

Writers need to consider mechanics and conventions as tools to lift their messages, clarify meaning, and focus their editing as they prepare for an audience.

Rereading is a tool that engages writers in processing print while supporting them at every phase of the drafting, revising, and editing processes. It is, unquestionably, our greatest tool for supporting the editing process.

- Writers need to reread constantly. They reread to confirm their message, to regain momentum, and to consider what to say next. They reread to think about organization and how their writing sounds. They reread to edit for spelling, punctuation, capitalization, and so on.

- Editing checklists guide writers in rereading for conventions and mechanics.

- Focused edits engage writers in a process of rereading once for each editing point.

Reread During Writing and Editing

DAY 1 Model the Focus Point

Rereading is one of the most important things that writers do. I reread while I am writing and, again, after I write. If I quickly reread, I can notice things that don't sound quite right and fix them immediately. Then when I am finished, I reread even more carefully! Let me reread my first few sentences: *Renewable energy comes from unlimited sources, such as sunshine, wind, and water.* I like my ideas and I feel good about the way the commas show the reader where to pause. In the second sentence, I used the word *harnessed*, but I am not sure if I used the correct spelling. I'll underline that word so I remember to check it when I reread to edit. [After writing] I have my ideas in place. Now I'll reread to edit. I need to double-check my grammar, spelling, capitalization, and punctuation. Rereading at this point is to fix mistakes.

> **Modeled Writing Sample**
>
> Renewable Energy
>
> Renewable energy comes from unlimited sources, such as sunshine, wind, and water. People have harnessed these sources throughout history. As long as 2,500 years ago, Greeks designed their homes to use winter sunlight for heating. For centuries, people have used wind to pump water and power ships. We still harness these sources today.

 TURN AND TALK I reread while I wrote, and I reread after I wrote. How were my two readings different? What was I looking for each time? How would this kind of rereading help you?

 SUM IT UP While you write, reread to focus on ideas and keep your train of thought. After you write, reread to proofread carefully and edit for mistakes in capitalization, grammar, punctuation, and spelling.

DAY 2 Guided Practice

Display student writing using a sample from the Appendix, like the one on page 180, or from your own class. If the author is one of your students, invite him or her to read aloud to the class.

 TURN AND TALK Discuss the meaning of the piece and think of a celebration to offer this author. Now, read over the writing. What suggestions might you have for this author?

 SUM IT UP To a class editing chart, add "Reread during and after writing."

Rereading is an important part of writing. During writing, focus on ideas. After writing, focus on using correct conventions and mechanics.

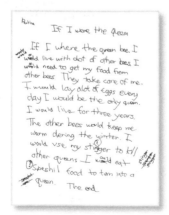

DAY 3   **Independent Practice**

Look through a writing folder to select a piece to reread for multiple purposes. Model how you think about meaning on a first reading and focus on proofreading and editing during a second reading. Allow time for student editors to proofread and edit their work.

 PEER EDIT Share the things you noticed about your writing as you read for the first and second time. Indicate places where you edited. Exchange and proofread each other's papers. Allow the writer to make any needed changes.

 SUM IT UP Writers reread their work to focus on meaning during writing and to proofread and edit after writing.

✔ Assess the Learning

- Use a class record-keeping grid as you observe editors at work. Document writers who revise ideas during writing and proofread and edit after writing.

- Ask editors to make a T-chart with two categories: *I can successfully proofread for. . .* and *These points are still a challenge. . .* Assess for understanding.

∞ Link the Learning

- Encourage students to read multiple times by having them tally each time they read. You might have them record their tallies on sticky notes placed on their desks.

- Model rereading several times as you create different types of writing. Continue to read first for the meaning and devote the final readings to careful proofreading and editing.

- Have students read outstanding examples of picture books at least twice. On the first read, have them focus on meaning and getting the gist. Then have them reread, looking very closely at conventions and mechanics, noticing the author's use of commas, transition words, spacing, end punctuation, grammar, and sentence structure. Provide an opportunity for readers to share their thinking about the writing they explored. Some outstanding picture books to consider: *Homerun* by Robert Burleigh, *Two Bad Ants* by Chris Van Allsburg, *Dogteam* by Gary Paulsen, *Shrek* by William Steig, *Wilma Unlimited* by Kathleen Krull, and *Punctuation Takes a Vacation* by Robin Pulver.

Use an Editing Checklist

Model the Focus Point

Note: You will need: (1) an enlarged copy of one of the editing checklists from the Assessment and Record-Keeping section, pages 165–166, to be displayed as a chart or on the overhead and (2) a piece of writing created in a previous modeled writing lesson.

> **Modeled Writing Sample**
>
> What has dry, scaly skin, four legs, a bony skeleton, and breathes air through its lungs? Reptiles. Many of us recognize lizards, snakes, turtles, alligators, and crocodiles as reptiles. Did you know that reptiles cannot generate heat within their own bodies? When you see a lizard sunning itself, it's absorbing heat from the sun.

An editing checklist helps me focus on the elements that make my writing strong. To use an editing checklist, I review a completed piece of writing, focusing on each point on the list, one point at a time. This checklist reminds me to start each sentence with a capital letter. The word *reptiles* after the first sentence is a fragment, but I still need to capitalize it. I better change *reptiles* to *Reptiles*. Spelling is the next item on my list. I want to check to see if *breathes* is correct. Now is the right time to turn to a resource because my writing is finished. I'll use a dictionary because I know that *breathes* isn't on the word wall of frequently-used words. My editing checklist includes end punctuation. Watch as I check each sentence to be sure it has the correct punctuation.

 TURN AND TALK How did the editing checklist help me focus on proofreading and editing? Why is it helpful to check on each editing point rather than reading for all editing points at the same time?

SUM IT UP After writing, use a checklist to proofread and edit for one item at a time to find and fix errors.

Guided Practice

Use the writing sample from page 188 or choose a selection from your class and display it on the overhead. If the author is one of your students, invite the author to read the selection.

> **A Harry Potter Book Review by Carlos M.**
>
> My favorite author is JK Rowling. Everyone knows she has written the Harry Potter books. She teaches us lessons about life and entertains us. I think she does a good job of developing her characters. Even Harry isn't perfect all the time. I've had some of his problems with friends and schoolwork.
>
> I am reading the fifth book, Order Of The Phoenix. If I was JK, I would have written these chapter titles:" The Order Begins"," Kids on a Mission","Lessons Learned", and " Fighting for Justice". I won't tell you which chapters they go with. You'll need to read the book and make a guess. Then will I let you know!
>
> Anyone want to have a Harry Potter book club? Let me know. I love to talk about Harry!

TURN AND TALK Discuss the meaning of the writing and give the author a specific compliment about the work. Distribute editing checklists. **Using your checklists, proofread for one item at a time, checking off items that have been addressed. Be prepared to offer suggestions to the writer.**

SUM IT UP To a class editing chart, add "Use editing checklists."

Remember, check one item at a time on the checklist as you edit.

DAY 3 Independent Practice

Model selecting a piece of writing from a writing folder. Remind students how to use the checklist to proofread and edit for one targeted point at a time. Student editors then use the checklists to proofread and edit, focusing on one point at a time.

 PEER EDIT Think about using the checklist to edit. How did using the checklist help you focus your editing? What edits did you make?

SUM IT UP Checklists are used at the end of writing to carefully check for one aspect of writing at a time. Editing checklists help you polish your writing for an audience.

✅ Assess the Learning

- Students can write letters to their parents explaining how to use a checklist to edit for one writing point at a time after writing is completed. Assess letters for student understanding.

- Use class grids to record information on your students' error patterns made by individuals. Study the patterns to establish the list of points to include on editing checklists or to identify writers who need additional instruction.

Link the Learning

- Volunteer your students to teach a class of younger writers how to edit with editing checklists. Have students devise checklists appropriate to the grade level and then teach their young partners how to use the checklists with their writing.

- Celebrate the role that checklists can play in crafting solid writing by posting examples of editing checklists and pieces of writing before and after the focused editing.

- Ask students how editing checklists would vary when used for different genres of writing, such as a newspaper story, a science learning log, a procedural text with numbered steps, and so on. As students write for different authentic purposes, work with them to create editing checklists to match the genre and purpose of the writing.

Use Copyediting Symbols

Model the Focus Point

Note: Prepare this writing in advance and have an enlarged copy of Copy Editor's Symbols from the Tools section, page 160, for the students to view.

> **Modeled Writing Sample**
>
> Dear Mr. Burliegh ⌃
>
> When I picked/up your book,
>
> Home Run, my heart skipped   u/l
>
> a beat. I coould'nt believe you ⌃had
>
> written about my favorit player   sp
>
> babe Ruth! Thank you for bringing   CAP
>
> him to life on the pages of your
>
> book ⊙

Have you ever noticed that the books we check out from the library usually don't have mistakes in them at all? That's because copy editors carefully look for mistakes in writing and fix them. Today, I am going to think like a copy editor and use copyediting symbols to show problems I find in the writing. Copyediting symbols make it easier for the author to fix the problems. This is a letter, and the greeting needs to end with a comma. To show the writer to insert a comma, I write a comma with a caret mark above it. The writer doesn't need a hyphen between *picked* and *up*, so I add this little squiggle—it means the writer should delete the hyphen. The book title needs to be underlined, so I draw a line under it and put the letters *u/l* in the margin. Here's a word that I know is misspelled. Putting this *sp* near the word shows the writer to fix the spelling.

👀 **TURN AND TALK** How might copyediting symbols help us make writing better? How can we use copyediting marks to help our writing partners?

☺ **SUM IT UP** Copy editors focus on errors that, when fixed, can make our strong writing even stronger. When we publish pieces, they need to be error-free so our meaning will be understood by our readers.

Guided Practice

Use the writing sample on page 178 or a piece of student writing to guide practice in using copyediting symbols. If the author of the piece is a student, invite him or her to read the selection to the class.

👀 **TURN AND TALK** Discuss the text's meaning and think of a compliment to share with the writer. Partners, it's time to think like copy editors. If you were editing this piece for the writer, what copyediting marks would you use?

Provide copies of the Copy Editor's Symbols from the Tools section, page 160.

SUM IT UP To a class editing chart, add "Use copyediting symbols to edit."

Copyediting symbols are signs that point the way to error-proof writing.

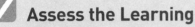 **DAY 3** **Independent Practice**

Make multiple copies of a piece of student writing, either from your class or from samples in this resource, and distribute to partners.

PEER EDIT Partners, work together as copy editors to prepare this piece of writing for a final, error-free copy. Insert copyediting symbols into the text. Be prepared to meet with another set of partners to explain your thinking and use of copyediting symbols.

SUM IT UP Copyediting symbols tell writers where they have made mistakes and how they should correct them. They lead to error-free final copies, a must for any published piece.

✅ Assess the Learning

- Observe students use of copyediting symbols to mark up their writing. Use your class record-keeping grid to record students' proficiencies.

- Gather writing samples that partners have edited using copyediting symbols. Assess your students' understanding.

🔗 Link the Learning

- Students can create posters to show copyediting symbols and present them as gifts to students in other classrooms.

- Create an authentic purpose for writing that needs to be polished in order to be published, such as letters to parents, articles for a school newsletter, articles for a school Web site, and so on. With the audience in mind, students should perfect their writing through the use of copyediting symbols.

- Students might enjoy teaching younger buddies how to use copyediting symbols. They can start with simple symbols, such as those for capitalization and end punctuation.

Cycles for Success With Capitalization

apitalization alerts readers and writers when words carry significance, when new sentences are beginning, or when a word is a proper noun or proper adjective. In fourth and fifth grade, writers often have gained control over using capitals at the beginnings of sentences and proper names. They are ready to branch out and explore a wider range of purposes for capitalization and to consider the way capitalized words are integrated into both their reading and their writing.

The Class Record-Keeping Grid: Capitalization, page 174, is especially helpful in monitoring your students' progress with capitalization. We encourage you to keep it handy as you circulate during writer's workshop or gather students for one-on-one conferences. With this tool at hand, you can quickly date the grid when you see evidence of a capitalization rule being followed or survey the grid to determine which students share a need for a capitalization review.

Class Record-Keeping Grid: Capitalization

	Proper nouns: people	Proper nouns: places	Proper nouns: things	Titles used with names (President Lincoln)	Abbreviations	Titles of books, magazines	Days and months	First word of direct quotation

Capitalize Proper Nouns

DAY 1 Model the Focus Point

In today's writing, I will focus on capitalizing the first letter of proper nouns. A common noun names a person, place, thing, or idea, such as *boy*, *city*, *cereal*, or *love*. A proper noun names a specific person, place, or thing, such as *Ted*, *Aurora*, and *Kellogg's Corn Flakes*. Proper nouns make writing strong, because they name specifics. I am writing about a famous person in U.S. history, Harriet Tubman. She was a slave. *Slave* is a common noun; it's not naming a specific person. She was born in America, a specific country, so it needs a capital letter. Harriet Tubman's name needs capital letters, too. I am going to write about an overseer, but I don't know the overseer's name, so I won't capitalize the word, *overseer*, because it's not his name.

> ### Modeled Writing Sample
>
> Born a slave in America, Harriet Tubman endured cruelty even as a young girl. When she didn't follow the order of an overseer, he injured her head so badly she suffered from headaches the rest of her life. Later, Tubman escaped to Canada. She returned to Maryland to help other slaves escape on the Underground Railroad.

TURN AND TALK Why did I need to capitalize *Canada*? Talk about one noun I capitalized and one noun that I didn't. Identify the reason that particular noun starts with a capital letter.

SUM IT UP The names of specific people, places, things, or ideas need to be capitalized, because they are proper nouns. Common nouns are not capitalized.

DAY 2 Guided Practice

Display a transparency or large chart of the Interest Inventory from the Tools section, page 162. Model filling out the first few lines, thinking out loud about which words are common nouns, which are proper nouns, and where capital letters should be placed. Distribute copies of the form to your students.

TURN AND TALK The purpose of this interest inventory is to gather information from your partner through an interview. Be very careful and think together about common nouns and proper nouns.

SUM IT UP To a class record-keeping grid, add "Capitalize proper nouns."

Remember, writers, we don't capitalize common nouns. But proper nouns that name specific people, places, things, or ideas need to begin with capital letters.

As you thumb through a writing folder, model how to select a sample that includes proper nouns. Show students how you proofread and edit, ensuring that those proper nouns are capitalized.

 PEER EDIT Share examples of both common and proper nouns in your writing. If your writing includes no proper nouns, think of a way that you can make your writing more specific by changing at least one common noun to a proper noun.

SUM IT UP We always capitalize proper nouns, but we never capitalize common nouns. Proper nouns name a specific noun. Common nouns are more general.

✓ Assess the Learning

- Gather the completed interest inventories and assess for understanding capitalization of proper nouns.

- During writing conferences, have students point out proper nouns and explain why they included them. Choose common nouns for students to turn into proper nouns.

Link the Learning

- Think of additional instances of capitalization for nouns to share with students.

  - Important words in titles and headings

  - Words used as names: *Mom, Dad,* and *Grandma,* for example, or *Angie went skating with Mom.* They are not capitalized when preceded by an article or possessive, such as *my mom, your dad,* and *our grandma. Angie went skating with her mom.*

- Proper adjectives are formed from proper nouns. For example, *a quilt made in America* is *an American quilt.* Provide opportunities for students to craft proper adjectives from other proper nouns such as English muffin, Hershey chocolate, Swiss cheese, or Nike tennis shoes.

- Students can search for and highlight proper nouns in newspapers and magazines. They might also suggest common noun equivalents of the proper nouns.

- Write common nouns on index cards. Give each student an index card and have each write corresponding proper nouns on the back of the card. Examples might include planet/Saturn, mountain/Mount Everest, city/Denver, day/Friday, month/June, magazine/*Time,* ocean/Pacific, lake/Lake Superior.

Capitalize for Emphasis

DAY 1   **Model the Focus Point**

When I want selected words to be read with great expression, I can capitalize all the letters. This tells my reader that these words need to be emphasized and read with gusto. The trick is to use this only once in a piece of writing. If you include too much, the reader doesn't pay as much attention to your special word. I am writing a poem about my brother learning to drive. I want to start with *No! Stop!* I am going to use an exclamation point for *No* and *Stop*. I want to save my all caps word for a bit later. My next two lines tell the reader what is happening. I don't think I am ready for an all caps word yet; I am saving that for the climax. *CRASH!* is the climax of the writing, the big moment when things don't work out. Here is where I need those capital letters. Let's read this together with gusto!

> **Modeled Writing Sample**
>
> No! Stop! Eyes widen in horror
>
> Dad grabs for the wheel
>
> Eek! Squeal. CRASH!
>
> Everyone okay?

 TURN AND TALK Writers, think about the ways I showed emphasis. What did you notice? Would you have chosen the same word to capitalize?

 SUM IT UP To emphasize certain words, writers can capitalize all the letters in a word or use an interjection followed by an exclamation point.

DAY 2   **Guided Practice**

Display the writing sample on page 180 or one from your class that illustrates the use of all capitals in a word. If the author is one of your students, invite the author to read the selection to the class.

TURN AND TALK Talk about the meaning of the writing; then, discuss a compliment you can offer the author. Think about using all capitals or interjections to show emphasis. Where might you insert those tools into this writing?

SUM IT UP Add "Capitalize for emphasis" to the class editing chart.

Remember, to show emphasis, writers can capitalize all the letters in a word or use an exclamation point to create an interjection.

Walk writers through the process of selecting writing and then revisiting it to add emphasis. Their goal is to reread to find places where they used or could use all capitals or insert an interjection to show emphasis.

 PEER EDIT Take turns pointing out specific examples of using emphasis in your writing. Share your thinking about why you made those specific decisions.

 SUM IT UP Writers can capitalize all the letters in a word or use an interjection followed by an exclamation point to show emphasis.

Assess the Learning

- Have writers select a piece of writing that includes adding emphasis by using capitalization and interjections. Meet with small groups and have them share their thinking as they selected words for emphasis. Assess understanding.

- Have students who are not using or who are overusing capitals or exclamation marks for emphasis flag these strategies in reading materials. Listen to their explanation of how these authors used capitals and exclamation points for emphasis.

Link the Learning

- Have students select a page in their writer's notebook to label "Show Emphasis." Their goal is to record capitalized words and interjections that they could use in their writing. Encourage them to utilize onomatopoeia, words such as *eek! screech! thud!*, in their lists. Have them search their own writing, picture books, newspapers, comic books, and graphic novels for examples to include in their notebooks.

- Ask your media specialist to help you collect picture books that use capitalization and interjections to show emphasis. Examples to consider: books by Mo Willems such as *Don't Let the Pigeon Drive the Bus* or David Shannon's *No, David!* Students also enjoy using sticky notes to add words in caps and interjections to wordless books, such as *Good Dog, Carl* by Alexandra Day.

- Once students become fluent (pacing, expression, phrasing, intonation, etc.) with the book and have practiced emphasizing key words, partners select picture books with exclamation points and/or capitalized words to read to K/1 students.

Capitalize Titles, Headings, and Some Abbreviations

DAY 1 | Model the Focus Point

Display and share several informational selections with titles and headings.

> As we saw in the resources I shared, informational writing has a title and often several headings as well. To help me organize my writing, I am going to create some headings for a report. For my title, I want my title to say, *Unique Features of Some States*. I will capitalize the first and last words and all other words that are important. That means I capitalize *Unique* for sure. I am not going to capitalize *of*, but I do need to capitalize *Some*. That is important to the title. Several abbreviations utilize capital letters. When we abbreviate the name of a state, we capitalize the abbreviation. Arizona is AZ. Washington is WA. Notice heading 3 where I used *D.C.* That is the abbreviation for the District of Columbia, a proper noun that I must capitalize as well.

Modeled Writing Sample	
Title:	Unique Features of Some States
Heading 1:	The Desert of Tucson, AZ
Heading 2:	The Active Volcano of Cougar, WA
Heading 3:	The Monuments of Washington, D.C.

 TURN AND TALK Imagine that two new students arrive and that you and your partner are responsible for explaining to them how to capitalize titles and headings. Decide what you would tell them.

SUM IT UP When writing titles and headings, use capitals for the first and last words and all other important words. Watch for abbreviations that require capitalization, too.

DAY 2 | Guided Practice

Display a writing sample from your class that includes titles and headings or use the writing sample on page 186. If the author is one of your students, invite the author to read the selection to the class.

 TURN AND TALK Share a compliment about the writing that you can offer the author. What can you say about the meaning of the selection? Think together about how the author used capitals in titles and headings. Were there any abbreviated state names? Did you notice the capitals used to abbreviate a name in the writing about Rosa Parks?

> **A True American Hero**
> **The Story of Rosa Parks**
>
> She wasn't a tall woman or a loud woman. She wasn't a woman who made a scene. She was a tired woman, riding a bus, heading home after a long days work.
>
> As the bus filled up, Rosa Parks sat quietly, until the bus drive told her that she needed to give up her seat to a white man. He expected this quiet black woman to follow his order, figuring that no black person would face jail just for a bus seat. He was wrong.
>
> Mrs. Parks decided to stand up for her rights by remaining seated. She was arrested and went to trial. But this quiet lady, Dr. Martin Luther King, and thousands of others changed America forever. They did it without violence. They had a dream and followed it. Mrs. Rosa Parks is a TRUE American hero. I thank you.

SUM IT UP To a class editing chart, add "Capitalize the first and last words and other important words in titles and headings."

Remember, writers capitalize most words in titles or headings. Be sure to watch for capitalization in abbreviations, too.

DAY 3 Independent Practice

Prepare an informational passage that could have headings added and model proofreading for proper capitalization of titles and headings and possible abbreviations. Ask the writers to look in their folders and select writing that includes or could include a title and headings. Give them a few minutes to proofread and edit for capitalizations of these text features.

 PEER EDIT Together, check over titles and headings for correct capitalization. Check for abbreviations of states, too. Those need capital letters!

 SUM IT UP Capitalize the first, last, and all important words in titles and headings, and watch for abbreviations. They often require capital letters.

✅ Assess the Learning

- Review students' reading logs and writing folders to see how they are progressing with correct capitalization of titles and headings.

- Review informational writing samples to check for capitalization in headings and confer with small groups to assess students' understanding of capitalization of abbreviations.

🔗 Link the Learning

- Provide each student with a sticky note to record a read-aloud book recommendation. Include title, author, and year published, using correct capitalization.

- Have students complete a research report that includes these elements: at least two resources, a title, a minimum of three sections with headings, a drawing with a caption, a labeled diagram, and a bibliography with titles, authors' names, location of publisher, and year published. Support your students as they learn about the correct use of capitalization.

- Have students review selected resources from science and social studies, examining capitalization of titles and headings, the table of contents, and index.

- Provide newspapers and have students discuss capitalization of titles, headlines, and headings in the newspaper.

Cycles for Lifting Punctuation

Well-designed punctuation controls the flow of a message, helps the reader understand nuances of meaning, and makes the texts we construct more interesting. Punctuation should not be limited to end–of–process corrections. Rather, we believe it should be recast as a tool we use to shape our thoughts. Our objective is to support writers in understanding that punctuation, when thoughtfully used, can lift the quality of writing. With this in mind, we coach writers to think about punctuation at two significant points in the writing process:

1. During drafting: Here punctuation turns our thinking toward creating interesting phrasing, adding onomatopoeia and sound words, stimulating emotion in the reader with exclamation marks, creating an interesting opener to follow with a comma, and so on.

2. During editing: This is where we reread for the proper use of conventions and ensure that we have applied punctuation that will help a reader navigate our work.

Above all, we focus on helping students apply their knowledge of punctuation in a wide variety of contexts.

End Punctuation: Period, Question Mark, and Exclamation Point

Model the Focus Point

There are four kinds of sentences: declarative, interrogative, exclamatory, and imperative. As writers, we need to use a variety of sentence types to create writing that is more interesting to readers. My first sentence is a declarative sentence, because it simply makes a statement. This sentence ends with a period. My next sentence shares strong feelings. It's an exclamation, and it ends with an exclamation point to give extra emphasis. My third sentence is imperative. This means it is a command, telling me to do something. Imperative sentences, depending on how strong the command, can end with a period or an exclamation point. You all know end punctuation for a sentence such as *Could it really be time to get up?*

Modeled Writing Sample

I knew I was staying up too late. But my book was great! If books could talk, this one would say, "Finish me. Just one more page!" Without warning, the shrill of the alarm hit me like a bucket of cold water. Could it really be time to get up? I whimpered, "It's TOO early."

TURN AND TALK Think about my sentences. What was the effect of using four different kinds of sentences? Think together. Can you name the four types and the punctuation for each? Can you give an example of each sentence type?

SUM IT UP Using different kinds of sentences adds interest and variety to our writing. Each type of sentence needs to end with a specific punctuation mark.

Guided Practice

Use the writing sample from page 180 or one from your class. If the author is one of your students, invite the author to read the selection aloud to the class.

TURN AND TALK Discuss the meaning of the text and offer a compliment about the writing. Talk about the types of sentences in the writing. Count the number that are declarative, imperative, exclamatory, and/or interrogative. How might you change a declarative sentence into an exclamatory or interrogative sentence? What are the benefits of doing so?

SUM IT UP To a class editing chart, add "Use a variety of sentences."

Using different types of sentences adds variety to writing. Declarative, interrogative, exclamatory, and imperative sentences need different kinds of end punctuation.

Select a writing sample from a writing folder and think aloud as you tally the sentence types on a chart, checking end punctuation for each sentence. Share an idea for changing a sentence from one type to another to add interest or action. Allow time for editors to examine the end punctuation and sentence types to add depth to their own writing.

 PEER EDIT Share a tally of how many sentence types you used in this piece of writing. Think together about some sentences you could change from one type to another. Be sure to add the correct end punctuation.

 SUM IT UP Using different sentence types adds interest and variety to your writing. Declarative sentences end with periods, interrogative with question marks, exclamatory with exclamation points, and imperative with periods or exclamation points.

✔️ Assess the Learning

- Collect writing folders to assess students' proficiency in punctuating each of the four sentence types correctly. Provide support for students who need additional practice.

- During writing conferences, ask students to identify instances where they have incorporated all four sentence types in their work.

🔗 Link the Learning

- Have students analyze a book they are currently reading independently and tally the sentence types represented on a few pages.

- Students can search in mentor texts for sparkling examples of each type of sentence. Have them copy the sentences onto sentence strips, clearly identifying the source, and then display their sentences on a class bulletin board, labeling each type and highlighting the end punctuation.

- Identify words that signal interrogative sentences. Have students list words like *who, what, when, where, why, how,* and so on. Create a poster of interrogative sentences with great beginnings.

- Search for imperative sentences in student work, in directions, in rules posted in classrooms and in the hallways. Create a rubric for writing imperative sentences that really work.

Punctuation in Dialogue

DAY 1   Model the Focus Point

Dialogue can make a story interesting, fun, exciting—just better to read! But we have to give speakers credit for what they say by punctuating the dialogue the right way. In creating dialogue, we need to follow four rules. First, use quotation marks around the things people say out loud. Second, capitalize the first word in the quotation marks. The third rule is to put end punctuation and commas inside the quotation marks. Fourth, identify the speaker. So let's look at some dialogue I wrote to see if I followed all four rules. Did you notice that I didn't use the word *said*? It's tempting to write that word for each piece of dialogue, but that word is overused. I want my writing to be more interesting than that, so I'll use different words to convey how each speaker says the words. Watch to see how I occasionally let you use the context to infer who is speaking. Good readers can do that. When I finish writing, I read twice. On the first reading, I read to make sure I'm satisfied with the ideas. Then I reread for correct punctuation.

> ### Modeled Writing Sample
>
> "Is it time for lunch yet?" whined Cameron.
>
> "Not yet," Mom murmured, "I'm busy."
>
> "But I'm hungry!" Cameron insisted.
>
> "Would you like to make lunch for the two of us?"
>
> "Good idea! I really am starving."

TURN AND TALK Restate the four rules of punctuating dialogue with your partner. Check to be sure I used each rule. Remember, however, that we don't have to identify the speaker every time if the context makes it clear who is speaking. Look at a favorite picture book or novel together and check out the dialogue. Does all the dialog conform to the rules I described?

SUM IT UP When you write dialogue—the exact words of speakers—there are four rules for punctuating that dialogue. Remember also, that you don't need to identify the speaker every time, if the context makes it clear who is speaking. Use interesting alternatives to *said*.

DAY 2   Guided Practice

Distribute copies of the writing sample, "Hip Hip Hooray" on page 179, or choose a piece written by a student.

TURN AND TALK Writers, talk about this writing first for meaning and then offer a compliment to the author. Next, reread, looking very closely at the dialogue. How did the dialogue expand your understanding of the main character? Was there enough dialogue? Was it punctuated correctly? Think together to be sure all four rules of dialogue are in place.

SUM IT UP To a class editing chart, add "Follow the four rules for punctuating dialogue."

Remember, dialogue means the exact words of a speaker. In a newspaper interview, this would be called a "quote." Follow the four rules of punctuating dialogue and work really hard to avoid overusing the word *said.*

DAY 3 Independent Practice

Look through a writing folder to find a piece of writing with dialogue or a piece that could benefit from the addition of dialogue. Think aloud about how to add dialogue. Writers should then select a piece of their own work that would benefit from the addition of dialogue.

 PEER EDIT Look over the writing with your partner. Share any places where you have added dialogue. Be sure you can identify the exact words of speakers in the piece. Check for all four rules of punctuation.

 SUM IT UP Dialogue can make your writing more interesting and precise. Be sure that you follow the four rules of punctuating dialogue.

✔ Assess the Learning

- Collect writing samples that include dialogue. Use the Class Record-Keeping Grid: Rules of Dialogue, on page 176, to record your students' progress in applying the rules of dialogue.

- Have students choose a passage from a mentor text that includes dialogue. Ask them to explain how the author followed the four rules for punctuating dialogue.

◉ Link the Learning

- Encourage students to brainstorm alternatives to *said.* Have them write their ideas on index cards or sticky notes. Condense their work into a chart that can be posted and used as a writer's reference tool.

- Type a familiar text that includes dialogue, omitting the punctuation. Editors can work together to punctuate the piece correctly.

- Teach rules for punctuation of dialogue with paragraphs—each time a different person speaks, a new paragraph begins.

- Introduce the rules for "interrupting" a quotation by putting the speaker's name in the middle of the quotation. "Hi!" squealed Anna. "I'm so happy you're here."

- Invite students to interview staff members at school or community members about an important topic, an event coming up, and so on. Students can write articles about the topic or event, including direct quotations using the rules of dialogue.

- Point out the difference between dialogue ("Don't play ball in the house," Mom told us) and indirect quotations (Mom told us not to play ball in the house). How are they punctuated differently?

Apostrophe: Contractions

DAY 1 **Model the Focus Point**

Note: Write on the board: *I can't wait to do some writing today!*

I just used the contraction *can't* instead of saying, *cannot*. I put the two words together and used an apostrophe to show that I had left out some letters. We use contractions in our speaking all the time. When we use them in writing, we just need to remember to put an apostrophe to show that letters are missing. I'm writing a math riddle, and I'm going to make a point of using contractions to show you how to place the apostrophe. In the first sentence, I want to say, *I will* but let's make it *I'll*. This removes the *w* and *i*. It is important to put an apostrophe in place of those letters. Let's continue to look for other places where I can use contractions.

> **Modeled Writing Sample**
>
> What's This?
>
> I'll measure a circle or go around the globe.
>
> I'm very well-rounded as you've been told.
>
> When I've finished,
>
> I'm back to where I began.
>
> _____
>
> Answer: A circumference

TURN AND TALK Writers, reread the riddle, substituting two individual words every time you see a contraction. What is the effect of using the contraction?

SUM IT UP Contractions combine two words into one by taking out a letter (or letters) and replacing it with an apostrophe.

DAY 2 **Guided Practice**

Display the writing sample on page 187 or a selection from a student author. The sample should include contractions or places where two words could be turned into contractions.

> By Darby
>
> Penguin Bodys
>
> Penguins are not your ordinarey birds. There feathers may look like fur, but thy are, in fact, feathers. There mostly black on top and white on there bellies. From the sky, the black looks like the bottom of the water and from below, there white bellies look like ice or just blend with the sky.
>
> Most other birds use there feathers to fly. Not the penguins. Thay can't fly but are good simmers. There long, outer feathers help keep the water out. Under the outer feathers is a layer of down. Anuther layer comes below the down. However, its not feathers, but blubber. The blubber helps them stay warm in the cold waters of Antarctica. Most birds wuoldn't want to live there.
>
> Short legs are set back on there bodys. This makes them sway back and forth when they walk. Some call this waddling. Thay look awkward on land. This is one reason why thay slide on there bellys. Once thay dive into the sea, there good divers, thay become gracefull.

TURN AND TALK Talk about a celebration to offer the author and discuss the meaning of the piece. Then think about contractions. Find a place to add a contraction or stretch a contraction out into two words, and reread. How does including a contraction change the "feel" of the text?

SUM IT UP To a class editing chart, add "Contractions—put an apostrophe in place of the missing letters."

Remember, when you form a contraction, put an apostrophe in place of the deleted letters in the new word.

DAY 3 Independent Practice

Model how to select and then edit a writing piece for contractions. Give student editors time to reread for contractions and correct their own use of apostrophes in pieces from their own writing folders. Encourage them to add contractions where appropriate.

 PEER EDIT Read each other's papers, checking for the correct use of apostrophes in contractions. Can you find a spot in your partner's paper where a contraction could take the place of two words?

 SUM IT UP A contraction can make writing sound more informal or conversational. Remember that you form a contraction by putting two or more words together, removing certain letters, and replacing the letters you omit with an apostrophe.

 ## Assess the Learning

- Ask students to pick out contractions in a favorite book and identify the base words for each.

- During writing conferences, assess each writer's ability to integrate and explain the use of contractions.

Link the Learning

- Students often confuse the contraction *it's* (it is) with *its* (possessive pronoun). Encourage them to write sentences in a section of their writer's notebook to help them remember that *it's* is a contraction and needs an apostrophe, while *its* is a pronoun, like *his* or *hers*, and is not punctuated with an apostrophe.

- Many contractions are homophones. Teach students to distinguish tricky word pairs such as *you're/your, they're/their, its/it's,* and so on. Encourage them to write sentences to help them remember the difference between the words.

- Students can work in teams to create charts of contractions. They should include the words used to make the contraction along with the contraction itself (e.g., *I had = I'd, They will = They'll*). After checking their work, students can post the chart.

- Have students do a quick write to explore their thinking on when writers should use contractions and when they should write words out fully. Provide time to share with partners or in small groups.

Apostrophe: Singular Possessive Nouns

DAY 1 Model the Focus Point

"Ownership" is a way of saying that something belongs to somebody. To show ownership in writing, we form a possessive. Form a possessive by adding *'s* to the end of a singular noun—a noun that names only one person, such as *Robert's game* or *the waiter's menu*. In my first sentence, I am talking about the life of an ant. I have the article *an*, which shows that there is only one ant, so I use the singular possessive. I add *'s* to the noun. In the next sentence, I am writing about the needs of one colony. Turn to your partner. How should I identify the possessive?

 TURN AND TALK State the rule for forming a possessive with a singular noun. Think of at least two examples and be ready to share them.

SUM IT UP To show that one person, thing, place, or idea owns something, simply add *'s* to the end of the word.

Modeled Writing Sample

Life Underground

You can sometimes see the very top of an anthill, but it is important to remember that most of an ant's life takes place underground. With miles of tunnels and hundreds of rooms, ants stay busy tending to the colony's needs. There's a job for each ant. The queen's job is laying eggs. A soldier's role is defending the colony.

DAY 2 Guided Practice

Choose a piece of writing to place on the overhead, either the writing sample on page 181 or a writing sample from your class. Invite a student author to read his or her text aloud.

 TURN AND TALK What are your thoughts about the meaning of the piece? Share a compliment with the author. Now, decide whether and where the author successfully used singular possessive nouns. How might you smooth out the writing by adding a possessive noun?

SUM IT UP To a class editing chart, add "Singular Possessive: Add *'s*."

Remember, it's simple to form singular possessive nouns—just add *'s* to the end of the noun.

Survey a writing folder to locate a sample that includes singular possessive nouns. Think aloud as you proofread for the *'s* at the end of singular possessive nouns. Ask writers to select from their folders and proofread a piece for singular possessives.

 PEER EDIT Look over each other's papers to verify use of *'s* for singular possessive nouns. Be sure to point out to your partner a place where a possessive might simplify the text.

 SUM IT UP Adding *'s* to the end of a singular noun shows that one person, thing, place, or idea owns something.

 Assess the Learning

- Have students select an assortment from their writing folders that includes singular possessive nouns. Collect and assess your students' understanding, and record your findings on a class record-keeping grid.

- Have students flag examples of singular possessive nouns in reading materials. Record their understandings.

Link the Learning

- A self-checking strategy: Teach students to cover up the apostrophe and anything that follows. If the remaining noun is singular, they have correctly used the *'s* rule.

- Explain the concept of shared possession. When the possession is shared by more than one noun, add *'s* to the last noun only. In the following sentence, there is one treehouse that is owned by two people. *Mary and Bob's treehouse is amazing!* Students create a T-chart with two columns. One column is used for examples of individual possession, such as *Mary's treehouse and Bob's fort are amazing!* The second column is used for shared possession, such as *Mary and Bob's treehouse is amazing!*

- Provide a transparency and pen to partners. Partners prepare and present sentences that include singular possessive nouns. Encourage students to write sentences with information from content areas, and then share their sentences on the overhead.

Apostrophe: Plural Possessive Nouns

DAY 1 — Model the Focus Point

We already know that if one boy owns a bat, we write a phrase for the singular possessive noun by adding *'s* to the noun. But what if there were more boys—like on a baseball team—who owned many bats? You would change the singular *boy* to the plural, *boys*. To make the possessive form, simply add an apostrophe (boys'). I am writing about penguins. But I'm not thinking of one particular penguin—I am thinking about many penguins. Their lives seem hard to me. Because I am talking about more than one penguin, I simply add an apostrophe to the end of the plural noun to make *penguins'*. In this sentence, I am writing about many birds. How do I form the plural? I'll read this through twice when I am finished: once just to be sure that it makes sense and a second time to be sure that I have correctly formed plural possessive nouns.

> **Modeled Writing Sample**
>
> Penguins' lives seem hard to me! These birds' abilities to withstand snow blowing at 50 miles an hour and temperatures that dip to 40 below zero are simply mind-boggling. More remarkable are the penguins' parenting skills. After the females' egg-laying jobs are finished, the dads' responsibility is to keep the eggs safe in the harsh winter for months at a time.

 TURN AND TALK Identify the plural possessive nouns in my writing in your writer's notebooks. Now take the plural possessives you found and change each of them into a singular possessive. How do these possessives look different? Think together about what writers need to remember about identifying possessive nouns.

SUM IT UP To show that a plural noun owns something, add an apostrophe to the end of the word that ends in *s*.

DAY 2 — Guided Practice

Display the writing sample on page 186, or one from your class that includes plural possessive nouns. If the author is one of your students, invite the author to read the selection to the class.

> **Proper Tooth Care...A MUST!!!**
> By David S. and Carolyn H.
>
> Do you want false teeth when you get old? Do you want root canals when your not even old? If you don't start taking better care of your teeth these could be your future!
>
> Kids' teeth should be in much better shape than they are. We interviewed kindergartens through fifth graders and your mouth would fall open and hit the ground if you heard what we heard!!
>
> Four out of every five kids went to bed WITHOUT brushing their teeth at least one night every week. Just think. All those germs spending a 10 hour recess in your mouth just wrecking your teeths' chance for a good healthy life.
>
> Even MORE alarming (we only checked with the 4th and 5th graders on this question) only one in 10 kids flossed! The dentists' opinion is that this is extremely important to get rid of plaque, which causes tooth decay too.
>
> We didn't even ask kids if they were eating junk food, we just watched and almost everybody did. We know that we should eat better, more fruits, vegetables, and less candy. This will help our teeth.

 TURN AND TALK Discuss a compliment for the author. What are your thoughts about the meaning of the selection? Review the procedure to make a plural possessive noun. How can you separate possessive nouns from contractions?

SUM IT UP To a class editing chart, add "Plural Possessive: Add an apostrophe to the plural noun."

When showing ownership by more than one person, place, thing, or idea, use an apostrophe at the end of plural nouns ending in *s*.

Look through a writing folder for a sample that includes plural possessive nouns or a sample where plural possessives could be added. Share your thinking as you proofread for the apostrophe and consider whether words are contractions or possessives. Now prompt writers to do the same with their own writing.

 PEER EDIT Together, look for examples of plural possessive nouns in each other's writing and verify that they are written correctly. Explain the ways in which plural possessives and singular possessives are different from each other. Make sure you aren't confusing contractions!

 SUM IT UP Adding an apostrophe to the end of a plural noun that ends in *s* makes the plural noun possessive.

✔ Assess the Learning

- Create a list of possessive nouns, both plural and singular. Ask partners to sort them and explain how they knew which were singular and which were plural.

- Ask students to point out singular and possessive nouns in their own writing. Ask them to explain how they know where to place the apostrophe in the possessive nouns.

∞ Link the Learning

- Have students rewrite a modeled writing sample that includes singular possessive nouns by turning them into plural nouns and their corresponding possessives.

- Partners can conduct a scavenger hunt for possessives and list each possessive on a card. Have them sort the possessives into singular and plural possessives after they have collected a nice selection, and then scramble the words and trade with another team.

- Students can work in teams to create rules posters for singular and plural possessive nouns. After checking posters for accuracy, post them in the room.

Comma: In a Series

DAY 1 Model the Focus Point

Note: Explain to students that a phrase is a group of related words that does not have a subject and verb, while a clause has both. *In constant motion* is a phrase. *Fingerlings glimmer* is a clause because both a subject and a verb are present.

> **Commas keep words from running together. They tell a reader where to pause and how to separate ideas. I am writing about seasonal changes in rivers. In my first sentence, I want to say, *rivers swirl, churn, and surge*. I am creating a series of three verbs. I need to separate them with commas and place the word *and* before the last verb in my series. Notice how the commas help me as a reader. They show me where to pause. This is also true when phrases or clauses are in a series. In sentence two I want to say, *otters play, deer drink peacefully, and fingerlings glimmer*. Notice how I use commas to separate the clauses in the series. When I'm finished, I'll reread to proofread and edit for commas separating words, phrases, or clauses in a series. I'll want to be sure I put *and* before the last idea in each list.**

> **Modeled Writing Sample**
>
> **Contrast**
>
> Ocean-bound rivers swirl, churn, and surge as they move toward the sea. In summer, otters play, deer drink peacefully, and fingerlings glimmer in the shallows. Winter storms transform the river to a raging torrent, sweeping rocks, trees, and even houses into its furious depth.

TURN AND TALK Think about how I used commas in a series. Explain how I used commas and what they tell the reader to do. Talk together about using *and*.

SUM IT UP We use commas between items in a series. They tell us where to pause. Remember to use the word *and* prior to the last item in a series.

DAY 2 Guided Practice

Place student writing on the overhead projector. Choose the writing sample on page 180 or one from your class that includes items in a series. If the author is one of your students, invite the author to read the selection to the class.

TURN AND TALK Discuss the meaning of the selection and offer a compliment to the writer. Now, think together about items in a series. Are there any places where commas should be added to separate items in a series? Is there any place where a series would strengthen the writing?

SUM IT UP To a class editing chart, add "Commas separate words, phrases, and clauses in a series."

Remember, commas separate items in a series and tell the reader to pause.

Model how to proofread a paper for commas in a series. Think aloud as you search so students see how you can insert items to create a series. Have writers choose a few selections from their writing folders where they used commas to separate words in a series or where a series could be created. Give them a few minutes to proofread and edit.

 PEER EDIT Show your partner where you used commas to separate words, phrases, or clauses in a series. Read your papers to each other with the commas and deliberate pauses. If you don't have a place where you have a series in your writing, create one in your writer's notebook.

 SUM IT UP Without commas to separate items in a series, readers wouldn't know when to pause.

✔️ Assess the Learning

- Use the Class Record-Keeping Grid: Commas, page 175, to monitor your students' use of commas in a series.

- Tell your students: "It is your responsibility to teach a new student to use commas to separate items or other groups of words in a series. Write out an explanation of what you would say to him or her. Include examples." Assess understanding.

Link the Learning

- Create teams of detectives who search for "Sentences With Words/Phrases/Clauses in a Series." Provide collections of familiar books and sticky note flags. Have teams flag sentences with items in a series. Then pair up teams to share their findings.

- Celebrate sensational sentences! Create a bulletin board titled, "Sentences With Noteworthy Items in a Series." Have teams write their favorite correctly spelled examples on sentence strips.

- Encourage readers to continue to read with writers' eyes. Have them record favorite sentences with words in a series in their writer's notebooks during sustained silent reading.

- Read *Alexander and the Terrible, Horrible, No Good, Very Bad Day* by Judith Viorst and notice how the author has used commas between adjectives in a list.

Comma: Compound Sentences

DAY 1 | **Model the Focus Point**

Note: Create a chart of connecting words (*so, or, but, and, for, nor, yet, while, finally*) that can join two complete sentences together.

When writers combine short, choppy sentences into longer, flowing sentences—it makes our writing sound much more sophisticated. Let's take a look at my sentences. *We were tied* **is very short so I will turn it into a compound sentence by linking it with the first sentence. Watch as I insert a connector and a comma.** *Rolf and I crossed the finish line together, so. . . .* **We need to be careful to choose connecting words that make the most sense and to include the comma when we connect the sentences.** *We waited* **is very short, too. I am going to make that into a compound sentence with** *The judges.* **Watch how I replace the period with a comma and use a connector to make these two sentences into a terrific compound sentence.** *Holding our breath, we waited, and the judges called us forward.*

> **Modeled Writing Sample**
>
> Rolf and I crossed the finish line together. We were tied. The judges pondered how to break the tie. We waited. We took a deep breath. We walked toward the judges' stand.

 TURN AND TALK What do you need to do to turn simple sentences into compound sentences? State the rule. Why might you include longer sentences in your writing? Should every sentence be a compound sentence? Tell why or why not.

 SUM IT UP Create a compound sentence by connecting two smaller sentences with a connecting word and a comma.

DAY 2 | **Guided Practice**

Place the writing sample from the Appendix, page 185, or one from your class on the overhead projector. If the author is one of your students, invite the author to read the selection to the class.

> Eddie #2
> Afterschool   Ms G   1-31
> Afterschool I like to play football with my dad. We play for a long time until we get bored. I sometimes play with a spongeball that you could throw over 100 yards, but it's hard to catch, and sometimes when were playing in the dark you just have to stick out your hands and hope you catch it but sometimes it will hit you in the head. It doesn't hurt though, because it made of sponge. Once I was playing in the dark and I threw the ball about 60 yards and hit him in the face.

 TURN AND TALK Discuss the selection's meaning and give the writer a compliment. Decide which sentences should remain as is, and which could benefit from being joined together to create compound sentences. Point out the connecting words and commas.

 SUM IT UP To a class editing chart, add "Compound Sentences: Join short sentences with a connecting word and a comma."

Our writing is more sophisticated when we vary sentences. Compound sentences, formed by combining two short sentences with connecting words and commas, add that sophistication and variety to our work.

Choose a sample from a student writing folder with compound sentences or with simple sentences that could be turned into compound ones. Model proofreading for compounds by thinking aloud about how to select a great connecting word, and then checking for a comma. Give the students time to identify compound sentences in their own writing or to create one by joining two short sentences.

 PEER EDIT Read and show each other your compound sentences. Together, try out different connecting words. Did you choose the best connecting word? Help each other find places where short, choppy sentences can be combined into compound sentences.

 SUM IT UP To create compound sentences, combine two short sentences with a connecting word and a comma.

✔ Assess the Learning

- Have students select compound sentences from their own writing to share with you during a writing conference. Assess their understanding and confirm that students understand they are not connecting phrases. They are connecting complete sentences.

- During independent reading time, ask students to collect examples of compound sentences from their reading. Assess to see if they have selected compound sentences and not sentences connected to a dependent clause.

⌘ Link the Learning

- Post compound sentences in a pocket chart. Using scissors, show students how each one remains a complete sentence even when separated from the other. Show them how to identify the subject and verb in each sentence, and then put the compound sentence back together again. With the sentences in the pocket chart, try inserting various connecting words to decide which connectors fit best.

- Have teams search for correlative conjunctions, conjunctions that are used in pairs, such as, "I'll *either* walk *or* catch a ride." Post these correlative conjunctions as a reference: *both/and*; *either/or*; *just/as*; *neither/nor*. Note that these are not compound sentences but structures that enrich our sentences with comparative thinking.

- Encourage students to collect terrific examples of compound sentences from literature and save them in their writer's notebooks and/or display them in the room for inspiration.

- In *Mechanically Inclined*, an excellent resource for middle school teachers, Jeff Anderson has created the acronym, FANBOYS, to refer to seven of the coordinating conjunctions: *for*, *and*, *nor*, *but*, *or*, *yet*, and *so*. We selected the four most often used, creating the acronym, SOBA!

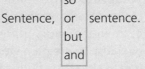

SOBA
Use a comma and a connecting word to connect sentences.

Sentence,	so	sentence.
	or	
	but	
	and	

Comma: After Introductory Phrase or Clause

Model the Focus Point

Note: Create a poster of starter words that can launch introductory clauses and post it.

To make my writing interesting and specific, I create sentences with different kinds of beginnings. Sometimes, I use starter words (*like*, *as*, *because*, *when*, *after*, *until*, *before*, *if*) to launch an introductory phrase or clause. It is important to notice the difference between a phrase and a clause. A phrase is a grouping of words that does not have both a subject and a verb. A clause does have a subject and a verb. Once I get the opener in place, I add a comma—that comma causes a natural "breath" when the sentence is read aloud. I'm writing a true story about a young boy who fell into a gorilla enclosure at the zoo. I am going to select *before* to launch my introductory clause. I know it is a clause because it has a subject and a verb. Now, I place a comma before continuing with *a perfectly regular day*. Notice how the comma sets my introductory clause apart and makes it noticeable. This draws a reader into the setting and helps the story flow smoothly. Introductory clauses also show transitions in time.

> ### Modeled Writing Sample
>
> *Before they knew it*, a perfectly regular day became a nightmare. *As the toddler's parents were watching a female gorilla and her baby*, the toddler climbed the zoo's railing and fell 20 feet onto the paved gorilla enclosure. *Moving quickly*, the gorilla scooped up the child and carried him to the zookeepers' door. *Because of the compassionate gorilla*, these parents will always remember this day at the zoo.

TURN AND TALK How did using openers affect my writing? Choose one of the starter words on the poster and create a new sentence that starts with an introductory phrase or a clause. Use sentence strips to record your sentence and be ready to share it. Be ready to tell if it is a phrase or clause.

SUM IT UP Begin sentences with introductory phrases or clauses to add variety and sophistication to your writing. Be sure that you include a comma after each introductory phrase.

Guided Practice

Use the writing sample, page 179, or a sample from your class that includes, or can be edited to include, commas following an introductory phrase or clause. If the author is one of your students, invite the author to read the selection to the class.

TURN AND TALK Consider a compliment for the author. Identify a place in the writing that could be strengthened with the addition of an introductory phrase. Could you use an introductory phrase or clause to create a stronger opening to the entire piece? If the writer already included introductory phrases or clauses, check to be sure that each one ends with a comma.

SUM IT UP To a class editing chart, add "Commas: Insert after an introductory phrase."

Remember, introductory phrases can make your writing more interesting and more specific. An introductory phrase or clause is usually followed by a comma.

 DAY 3 Independent Practice

Select a writing sample from a writing folder and share your thinking about introductory phrases and clauses. If there are none, look for places where they could be added. If phrases and clauses are included, think aloud as you check to see if they end with commas. Have writers take over the process by doing the same in their own writing.

 PEER EDIT Share your introductory phrases and clauses and check to see if they are followed by commas. Reread to think together about additional places where introductory phrases and clauses would add sophistication and specificity to the writing. Look carefully at your leads.

 SUM IT UP Introductory phrases and clauses make writing sound smoother and more sophisticated.

✅ Assess the Learning

- Confer with writers to assess their understanding of using commas after introductory phrases or clauses.

- During small-group instruction, assess your learners' ability to identify an introductory phrase and clause followed by a comma in their reading selections.

🔗 Link the Learning

- During your read-alouds, point out powerful introductory phrases and clauses by rereading them and recording them on sentence strips. Some examples to consider: *Wilma Unlimited* by Kathleen Krull, *Chicken Sunday* by Patricia Polacco, *Drummer Boy* by Ann Turner, *Animals Nobody Loves* by Seymour Simon, *Stone Fox* by John Reynolds Gardiner. Notice whether or not the author follows the opener with a comma.

- Do a modeled writing for the students showing how you can empower writing in social studies by consciously inserting introductory phrases or clauses, followed by commas.

- Have students create a section in their writer's notebooks for starter words that launch introductory phrases and clauses. Collect openers that they find while reading.

- Take a passage from a well-written text and strip away the introductory phrases or clauses. Post it on the overhead or on a chart and have students compare it with the original.

Comma: Before Closer

DAY 1   Model the Focus Point

A strategy for adding interest and variety to sentences is the use of a closer. Just like its name implies, a closer ends a sentence using a phrase that needs to be set off from the rest of the sentence with a comma. A comma makes a natural pause in the sentence and draws attention to the closer. In this first sentence, *peering curiously at a butterfly* is a closer. It's not a sentence all by itself, so when I use it as a closer, I need to put a comma after the words that make up the main part of the sentence. Do you notice how several of my closers begin with an /ing/ word. This is a helpful way to get started using closers. Sentences with closers are more interesting and stimulate sensory images. Close your eyes and visualize as I read this aloud. Notice how I will pause at the comma just before each closer. If I were writing this for a real audience, I wouldn't have my sentences all sound so much the same. We know that the best writing uses a variety of sentence structures to keep the interest of a reader. These are examples to help us learn how to include closers in our writing.

> ### Modeled Writing Sample
>
> The cat crouched low to the ground, peering curiously at a butterfly.
>
> The butterfly fluttered around the bush, landing on bright green leaves.
>
> The leaves ruffled in the wind, shimmering in the last light of the day.

TURN AND TALK Writers, what do you notice about the closers? What do they add to the writing? Try reading the writing without the closers to think about how the closers affect the meaning.

SUM IT UP Use closers to add more detail and sophistication to your writing. When you add a closer, precede it with a comma.

DAY 2   Guided Practice

Place student writing on the overhead projector. Use the writing sample from the Appendix, page 186, or from your class. If the author is one of your students, invite the author to read the selection to the class.

> ### A True American Hero
> ### The Story of Rosa Parks
>
> She wasn't a tall woman or a loud woman. She wasn't a woman who made a scene. She was a tired woman, riding a bus, heading home after a long days work.
>
> As the bus filled up, Rosa Parks sat quietly, until the bus drive told her that she needed to give up her seat to a white man. He expected this quiet black woman to follow his order, figuring that no black person would face jail just for a bus seat. He was wrong.
>
> Mrs. Parks decided to stand up for her rights by remaining seated. She was arrested and went to trial. But this quiet lady, Dr. Martin Luther King, and thousands of others changed America forever. They did it without violence. They had a dream and followed it. Mrs. Rosa Parks is a TRUE American hero. I thank you.

TURN AND TALK Discuss the purpose of the writing. Decide on a compliment for the author. Identify and reread the closers. Check each for a preceding comma. Discuss ideas for additional closers.

SUM IT UP To a class editing chart, add "Comma: Insert before sentence closers."

Remember, writers choose to end sentences with closers to add specific details and to make writing more interesting. A closer is set off from the rest of the sentence by a comma.

DAY 3 **Independent Practice**

Select a sample from a writing folder to edit for closers. Model how you check to be sure that commas precede closers. If no closers exist, share your thinking as you find places where adding a closer would lift the writing. Writers can follow your example by adding more closers to their own work. Remind students that adding one or two closers to a piece of writing is often enough. Sentence variety is really important.

 PEER EDIT Take turns reading your writing, identifying closers and checking to be sure that commas precede them. Then, suggest to your partner a place to add a closer.

 SUM IT UP Using closers at the end of sentences is a technique to bring sophistication to writing. Be sure to insert a comma before the closer.

 Assess the Learning

- Collect student writing samples that include closers. Assess to see that closers are always preceded by a comma. Use the Class Record-Keeping Grid: Commas, on page 175, to note which students use a comma prior to the closer.

- Ask readers to flag examples of closers in their reading. Check for student understandings.

Link the Learning

- Generate a poster of *-ing* verbs (participles), such as: *running, wishing, clinging*, and so on, to post as a resource for writers. Participles can be helpful beginnings for openers as well as closers.

   Example of a closer: *I finished the laundry, <u>wishing I were soaking in the tub</u>.*

   Example of an opener: *<u>Wishing I were soaking in the tub</u>, I finished the laundry.*

- Have your students become sentence collectors, searching for sentences that use participles as openers and closers. Encourage them to savor these sentences in a special section of their writer's notebooks. Make conscious use of these sentences across the curriculum, and celebrate when writers use powerful openers and closers.

- During small-group reading instruction, guide students in reading like a writer to discover and celebrate openers and closers.

- During independent reading, have students keep their writer's notebooks open so they can note terrific openers and closers when they find them. Encourage them to record the source, the page number, and the sentence.

Comma: Separating an Interrupter

DAY 1 — Model the Focus Point

As I write about watching skateboarders in a half-pipe, my first sentence begins, *The first skater, a boy of eleven, stands...* Did you notice how I added information to explain who the first skater is by placing a descriptive phrase in the middle of the sentence? This technique is called an *appositive*, also known as an *interrupter*. True to its name, it interrupts a sentence right in the middle, so it needs to be set off from the sentence with two commas. Notice how the interrupter adds information about the skater. Interrupters clarify, add information, or even rename things. In my second sentence, I will place the interrupter closer to the end, *catches big air*, more than three feet, *before...* Again, notice how the interrupter adds information. It tells how much big air. Let's read this together and emphasize the interrupters when we read them.

> ### Modeled Writing Sample
>
> The first skater, *a boy of eleven*, stands on the coping and then blasts into the drop. He charges up the other side of the ramp and catches big air, *more than three feet*, before turning and blazing back into the pipe.

TURN AND TALK Writers, what do you notice about the interrupters? What do they add to the writing? Read a sentence without the interrupter. Notice that I can cover the interrupter with my hands and the sentence is still complete.

SUM IT UP Use interrupters to rename a noun or add more detail and sophistication to your writing. When you add an interrupter, set it off with commas. Interrupters clarify and add information, but they are not sentences.

DAY 2 — Guided Practice

Place a copy of the Harry Potter book review, on page 188, on the overhead and show students how you can easily insert an interrupter that renames something or tells more about it. Example: Harry Potter and the Deathly Hallows, *the newest Rowling adventure*, is not only..."

> **A Harry Potter Book Review by Carlos M.**
>
> My favorite author is JK Rowling. Everyone knows she has written the Harry Potter books. She teaches us lessons about life and entertains us. I think she does a good job of developing her characters. Even Harry isn't perfect all the time. I've had some of his problems with friends and schoolwork.
>
> I am reading the fifth book, Order Of The Phoenix. If I was JK, I would have written these chapter titles:" The Order Begins"," Kids on a Mission","Lessons Learned", and " Fighting for Justice". I won't tell you which chapters they go with. You'll need to read the book and make a guess. Then will I let you know!
>
> Anyone want to have a Harry Potter book club? Let me know. I love to talk about Harry!

TURN AND TALK Writers, think together. Find places where we could add interrupters to this piece to add clarity. Look for places where you can rename something or tell more.

SUM IT UP To a class editing chart, add "Interrupters are framed with commas."

Remember, writers use interrupters to add information and make sentences richer. Interrupters are framed by commas.

DAY 3 | **Independent Practice**

Think aloud as you select a sample from a writing folder and consider adding interrupters. Model how you check to be sure that commas frame the interrupter. Writers can follow your lead to add interrupters to their own work.

 PEER EDIT Talk to your partner about places where you have added interrupters to your writing, and be sure you have used commas to frame them. Help each other think of more interrupters that you might add.

 SUM IT UP Using interrupters in the middle of sentences brings sophistication and clarity to writing. Be sure to insert commas around interrupters.

✅ Assess the Learning

- Have students collect four examples of sentences with interrupters from their own writing and from their reading selections. Assess their understanding from their samples.

- Use the Class Record-Keeping Grid from the Assessment and Record-Keeping section, page 175, to indicate which students are placing commas around interrupters.

∞ Link the Learning

- Create Readers Theater sentences . . . with interruptions. Have two students take responsibility for sentences with interrupters. One student reads the majority of the sentence, the other dramatically reads only the interrupter.

- Conduct a search for great interrupters! Have students collect spectacular examples of sentences with interrupters on sentence strips. Post their examples in a highly visible place to fuel their use of interrupters in their own writing. Here are some examples to get them going:

    > The dog, eyes rolling and ears flopping, plunged through the bushes in a frantic dash for escape. Our teacher, Mr. Allenton, thrills us with examples from his own writing. The bullets of hail, stinging and cold, burned into exposed flesh. The cabin, a rugged and ancient building, hung perilously atop the mountain.

- During small-group reading instruction, guide students in reading like a writer to discover and celebrate interrupters.

Comma: Transition Words to Show Passage of Time

DAY 1   Model the Focus Point

Note: Post a chart of transition words. See Tools section, page 155.

> As I write about turtles today, I am going to focus on transition words that show changes in time. Words like *once*, *while*, *soon*, *then*, and *next* all help to show that time is moving forward. These transition words are helpful tools for a writer. When I use a transition word or phrase, I often follow it with a comma. My first sentence starts, *Once in the spring. . . . Once* is my transition word. Notice that I add a comma after *spring*, because that is the end of the phrase telling when. The comma is really important. Next, I need a transition word that tells that a bit of time has passed.
>
> I will use *while* to show that two things are going on at the same time. Transition words really help me to show time and setting. Let's reread to see how I am doing with my transition words. Good writers and editors reread all the time.

> **Modeled Writing Sample**
>
> Once in the spring, a female turtle lays more than a hundred eggs. While the eggs settle, she gently spoons sand over her nest. Meanwhile, the tiny turtles mature and prepare to hatch. Soon, tiny turtles will begin to work their way toward the sea.

 TURN AND TALK Using the posted list of transition words, find transition words in my example. Are there any other transition words that I could have selected? If I were to keep going, which transition words would help me continue?

SUM IT UP Use transition words to alert the reader that time is moving forward. A comma usually follows a transition word or phrase.

DAY 2   Guided Practice

Display the writing sample on page 189 on the overhead and show the students how you can slip transition words into the piece, in place of other sentence openings.

TURN AND TALK Discuss the meaning of the selection and plan a compliment for the writer. Think together about transition words. Identify them and explain the benefits of using transition words.

> **The Heart**
>
> With unrelenting consistency, the muscles of the heart squeeze together. These contractions of the heart are so powerful they could send a jet of water six feet high into the air. Each time the muscles contract, blood surges through the chambers of the heart gathering speed, pulsing with power. As the blood pushes out of the left ventricle of the heart, it smashes with great force into the aorta, the blood vessel that directs blood away from the heart and toward the rest of the body. Deep and fast, blood streams into ever-smaller tunnels. Shivery and quick, blood travels into veins and capillaries delivering oxygen and nutrients to needy cells.

SUM IT UP To a class editing chart, add "Use transition words to show passage of time. Follow them with a comma."

Transition words alert the reader that time is moving forward or backward.

DAY 3 **Independent Practice**

Post a chart of transition words. Select a writing sample from a student folder to proofread for use of transition words. Ask students to select writing and to proofread for transition words followed by commas. If their writing doesn't include transition words, have them edit to include them.

 PEER EDIT Take turns identifying transition words and explaining their function in sentences. Then, read the writing with the transition words and without. Decide which makes the writing stronger. Help each other add transition words to show the passage of time.

 SUM IT UP Remember, writers use transition words to tell the reader that time is passing. Transition words are usually followed by commas.

 Assess the Learning

- Gather writing folders and assess to see which students are integrating transition words into their writing.

- Have students identify and collect transition words in their reading selections.

Link the Learning

- Read *Wilma Unlimited* by Kathleen Krull, once to enjoy this amazing biography and a second time to identify the transition words.

- Send the students on a scavenger hunt for transition words in resources they use for independent reading, small-group instruction, and content area investigations.

- Have writers use their writer's notebooks to experiment with using a variety of transition words and phrases that begin with a transition word. They may want to create a rich list of transitions to keep for ready reference as well as collect great sentences from literature.

- Provide copies of Create Your Own Resource: Transition Words, page 155. Have students complete it and then insert the resource into their writer's notebooks after you have assessed their understanding.

Cycles for Improving Grammar Awareness

"A word of caution: Some grammar programs teach rules in isolation. Research has shown this is a detached and futile exercise."
—*Donna Hooker Topping and Sandra Josephs Hoffman*

R ead-alouds and the rich conversations we have with learners all day long are essential building blocks of grammar development. With mentoring from the authors we love, our ears become tuned to what "sounds right." We come to expect certain sentence structures and notice when nouns and verbs do not agree. We notice when plurals are missing or tense is misplaced. When we *float learning on a sea of talk*, we maximize the potential for grammar and oral language development.

Modeled writing enables students to hear us wonder aloud about pronoun choices, verb tenses, word order, and so on. When students can see a proficient language user in action, they begin to see how to integrate the writing strategies we're teaching into their work as writers.

When focusing on grammar, take cues from your students. Listen to how they speak and look closely at the grammar embedded within their writing samples. Pay special attention to English learners and to students who come from homes where nonstandard English is spoken. With careful observation of the language patterns that are already in place, you can direct their attention to the structures and forms that are woven into read-alouds, as well as elaborate on and extend what students say. For example, if a student says, *I seen a car wreck,* your response might be, *You saw a car wreck! I hope everyone was okay.* This elaboration and expansion of language supports and stretches learners.

Complete Sentences vs. Fragments

Complete sentences have at least two parts, and a great way to find them is to ask: (1) Who or what did something? (2) What did they do? Complete sentences always have both of these parts. A fragment is a group of words missing one of these parts. My first group of words is *The stars twinkled in the sky*. Let's check for a subject. The subject is *the stars*. What did the stars do? They *twinkled in the sky*. This group of words has both parts—it's a complete sentence. Now look at my next group of words. *The pinpricks of light on a vast dark blanket*. We need to ask our two key questions. I am looking for "who or what did something," and I see a noun phrase—*pinpricks of light*. What did the pinpricks of light do? Oops. This is a fragment. To fix the fragment, I will rewrite this sentence to say, *The pinpricks of light on a vast dark blanket drew the attention of my telescope*. Partners, think together. Did this rewritten sentence answer both of our key questions?

> **Modeled Writing Sample**
>
> The stars twinkled in the sky. Like pinpricks of light on a vast dark blanket. Galaxies sprang into focus. The brilliance of the Milky Way.

TURN AND TALK Partners, think together. What are the two key questions to use in checking for complete sentences? How will you help yourselves remember to use them?

SUM IT UP A sentence requires two parts: a subject (who or what did something) and a verb (what they did). If you have a fragment, you can add the missing part to make a sentence.

Place student writing on the overhead projector. Use the writing sample from the Appendix, page 189, or one from your class. If the author is your student, invite the author to read the selection to the class.

> **Arthropods: The Crayfish**
>
> The crayfish has a fairly complicated nervous system that helps it control movement as well as its senses. The system runs the entire length of the body with a ganglion, a small localized "brain," controlling each segment of the body. A collection of ganglion. The head region has many ganglion that control the others around the body.

TURN AND TALK Talk about the meaning of the writing. Share a specific compliment you could give the author. Identify sentences by looking for subjects and verbs. Ask the two critical questions. Do you find any fragments in the writing? Make a plan for turning those fragments into sentences.

SUM IT UP To a class editing chart, add "Complete sentence = subject + verb."

Remember, a sentence answers two critical questions: Who or what did something? What did they do?

DAY 3 **Independent Practice**

Have students gather their writer's notebooks and select a few pages to review. Remind them that a complete sentence includes both a subject and a predicate. Have students review the selected pages, identifying the subjects and verbs of sentences. If students' writing includes fragments, challenge them to correct their fragments by adding the missing part.

 PEER EDIT Read a complete sentence from your writing to your partner so that your partner can identify the subject and the verb. Then select a sentence from your partner's writing that you think is especially strong. What makes that sentence a powerful one?

 SUM IT UP A complete sentence has two parts: the subject and the verb. The subject identifies the "who" of the sentence, while the verb tells what the subject did. If you have only one of these parts, the group of words is a fragment, not a sentence.

✅ Assess the Learning

- Students use Editing Checklist II or III, on pages 164–165, to assess their own papers for complete sentences. Track students' improvement in writing complete sentences.

- During writing conferences, have your students demonstrate how they look for both a subject and predicate to be sure that they have written complete sentences.

🔗 Link the Learning

- Students flag sentences that "speak to them" from their silent reading books. Partners share flagged sentences and the reasons for their selection. Then, students identify the two basic components of each sentence.

- During silent reading, have students select a sentence or two to "test" by identifying the subject and the predicate. They can record their selected sentences to share with classmates.

- Invite students to place their favorite sentences on index cards. Pair students up. Partners read each other's sentences and identify the subjects and verbs.

- Point out that not all fragments are "bad." Although they are not generally used in formal writing and should never be used on a writing assessment, fragments can break up sentences and can build imagery or suspense in writing. You might choose to focus on a few books that make good use of incomplete sentences. Gary Paulsen's *Dogsong* or Robert Burleigh's *Homerun* are wonderful texts for examining the poetic effects of deliberately placed fragments.

Sentence Openers: Adverbs and Adverb Phrases

DAY 1 **Model the Focus Point**

Adverbs and adverb phrases tell readers where, when, how, and to what extent. These phrases help pull readers right into the setting. I want my reader to join me on the edge of a cliff, so I will use an adverb phrase followed by a comma to begin. *At the stroke of midnight, Inez walked to the edge of the cliff...* Close your eyes and visualize. What is it like, creeping along a cliff's edge at midnight? Probably dark and maybe a little scary! Watch as I underline the adverb phrase I used to open that sentence. In sentence two, I will open with another adverb, but this time I will use a single adverb, *quickly*. Notice how I place a comma after *quickly*. When we open with an adverb or an adverb phrase, we often need to place a comma before the rest of the sentence.

> **Modeled Writing Sample**
>
> At the stroke of midnight, Inez walked to the edge of the cliff. Quickly, she looked back to see if anyone was following. Carefully, she edged closer. Looking down, she saw them peering up through the mist. Quietly, she reached into her pocket to retrieve her camera.

TURN AND TALK Adverbs and adverb phrases tell us *how, when, where,* and *to what extent*. Single adverbs work with verbs to add clarity and meaning to our writing. A word that ends in *-ly* is often an adverb. Find adverbs in my writing. See if you can also find adverb phrases.

SUM IT UP Adverbs and adverb phrases answer the questions *how, where, when,* and *to what extent something was done*. Single-word adverbs usually end in *-ly*.

DAY 2 **Guided Practice**

Display a writing sample, such as the one on page 185 or a sample from one of your students. Student authors may wish to read to the class.

TURN AND TALK Discuss the meaning of the writing and prepare a compliment for the writer. Notice the adverbs and adverb phrases that open the sentences. What do the adverbs add to the writing? Can you find a place where an adverb or adverb phrase could make the writing clearer or more interesting?

> **A Bum Rap**
> By B. B. Wolf
>
> I may be known as the Big Bad Wolf (B.B. for short). But I got a bum rap and I am here to tell you how it really went down...
>
> Slowly strolling along, my brother Al and I were out exercising his pet pig, Porkie. My brother he likes pigs a lot so he has always got a few of them wandering around in his yard for company. As we meandered along minding our own business, this really bossy mama pig comes raging up and demands that we come and help her kids. She says they are trapped in their house and need someone to help get them out.
>
> Quickly, me and my brother grabbed Porkie and went racing to the pigs' house. Just like that bossy mama said, there were three pig faces in the window looking scared as can be and the door was stuck tight.
>
> With a huge puff of shared wolf-power my brother and I we huffed and we puffed and we blew as hard as we could. Sure enough that house blew down and there sat three confused looking little pigs.
>
> You can imagine how surprised we were when the police came roaring up and threw Al and me in jail.

SUM IT UP To a class editing chart, add "Adverbs and adverb phrases are great sentence openers."

Adverbs and adverb phrases can create a clear picture for your readers by telling *when, where, how,* or *to what extent.*

DAY 3 | **Independent Practice**

Have students search through their notebooks and writing folders for writing that they can enhance with sentence-opening adverbs and adverb phrases. Give them a few minutes to proofread and edit.

 PEER EDIT Take turns reading your papers and pointing out places where you used adverbs and adverb phrases as sentence openers. Check for commas after your opening phrases. What single adverbs ending in *-ly* did you include?

SUM IT UP Adverbs and adverb phrases make powerful sentence openers. Use these tools to bring your reader right into your setting. Follow these openers with commas!

✓ Assess the Learning

- Survey writing samples to identify which writers understand how to use adverbs and adverb phrases as sentence openers. Provide additional support for those students who need it.

- Observe writers at work and ask them to point out places where they have included adverbs and adverbial phrases as openers. Ask them whether these adverbs and phrases tell *where, when, how,* or *to what extent* (*very, far, almost, really*). Confer with a writer as he or she finds a place to insert an adverb or adverb phrase.

∞ Link the Learning

- Have fun with adverbs in *Dearly, Nearly, Insincerely: What Is an Adverb?* by Brian Cleary and Brian Gable and *Up, Up, and Away: A Book About Adverbs* by Ruth Heller.

- Provide students with a copy of Create Your Own Resource: Understanding Adverbs and Prepositional Phrases, page 157, and have them complete it to add to their writer's notebooks.

- Adverbs often end in *-ly*. Have writers think together and make a list of *-ly* words to keep in their writer's notebooks. Here are some adverbs that do not end in *-ly*: *not, never, very,* and *always*. Also, caution students that some adjectives, such as *lonely, lively,* and *lovely* end in *-ly*. Adjectives describe nouns or pronouns, while adverbs describe a verb (*quietly ran*), an adjective (*extremely old*), or another adverb (*very quietly*).

Verbs: Powerful Descriptors

DAY 1 — **Model the Focus Point**

Note: You will need a copy of *Caves* by Stephen Kramer or another selection with rich verb selections.

Caves is a terrific resource for writers because of the verbs Stephen Kramer has so carefully selected. He proves that verbs can deliver more powerful descriptions than adjectives or adverbs if we focus on them as tools in our writing. As I read the first few pages to you, focus on the verbs, the action words, and visualize. Now, let's look at this example from page 6. The verbs are missing, so we are challenged to think like our mentor, Stephen Kramer, and select jaw-dropping verbs for these sentences. In the first sentence, I am thinking about *shatter the stillness*. I like the image I get with that verb. Think together: what other verbs might help this sentence to shimmer with imagery?

> **Modeled Writing Sample**
>
> From *Caves* by Stephen Kramer, page 6.
>
> Then, one day, footsteps _____ the stillness. Voices _____ through the air. Flashlight beams _____ across the darkness, lighting up a strange and wonderful sight. Stone icicles _____ overhead.

 TURN AND TALK What do you notice about the verbs we have selected and the meaning you get from the passage? How do the verbs help you understand the action in the piece?

SUM IT UP Verbs are sometimes called the engines of sentences. We need to make very careful choices and use verbs that spark sensory images for our readers.

DAY 2 — **Guided Practice**

Display *The Heart*, on page 189, on the overhead, then read it aloud dramatically.

TURN AND TALK Discuss the meaning of the passage, and share a compliment about the writing. Return to the passage and identify the verbs. What are the strengths of these verbs? Describe the imagery they create. What can we learn from this mentor text?

> **The Heart**
>
> With unrelenting consistency, the muscles of the heart squeeze together. These contractions of the heart are so powerful they could send a jet of water six feet high into the air. Each time the muscles contract, blood surges through the chambers of the heart gathering speed, pulsing with power. As the blood pushes out of the left ventricle of the heart, it smashes with great force into the aorta, the blood vessel that directs blood away from the heart and toward the rest of the body. Deep and fast, blood streams into ever-smaller tunnels. Shivery and quick, blood travels into veins and capillaries delivering oxygen and nutrients to needy cells.

SUM IT UP To a class editing chart, add "Verbs: Powerful Engines of Imagery."

Using a writer's notebook, select a sample to model proofreading for vivid verb selection. Think aloud about the verbs you find and alternatives that might add strength to the writing. Have writers review their own work to analyze verbs and prepare for a peer editing meeting.

 PEER EDIT Show your best verbs to your editing partner. Think together about other places in your writing where better verbs would strengthen the writing.

 SUM IT UP Powerful verbs elevate our writing, making it sparkle with energy and imagery.

✔ Assess the Learning

- Have students review independent reading selections and find at least five sentences with powerful verb choices. Have them record their sentences and the source in their writer's notebooks. Review the notebooks to assess for understanding.

- During a writing conference, pinpoint a sentence with a lackluster verb and ask the student to improve the verb choice.

Link the Learning

- Provide sentence stems without verbs and have partners work together to create the richest, most intense sentences they can. Example: The hungry giant _____ as he _____. The fragile butterfly _____ as it _____.

- Challenge partners to take a lackluster paragraph from a science book and rewrite it so that it has sparkling verbs that add rich meaning and energy. Use *The Heart* by Seymour Simon or *A Drop of Water* by Walter Wick as possible mentor texts.

- Have students use sentence strips to collect sentences with terrific verbs, then post the strips in a highly visible place as mentors to their writing.

Verb Tenses: Present, Past, and Future

DAY 1   **Model the Focus Point**

Verbs are remarkable. They show action or state of being, and they can show when something happens. The "when" part of the verb is called *tense*. We use three main tenses in our writing. The present tense describes something that is happening now. In my first sentence, I am describing something I know how to do. I use the present tense form of the verb. I am writing about something I do now—*I walk to school*. That takes place in the present, so I use the present-tense verb. In my next sentence, I am talking about something that happened a while ago. That means I need to use a past-tense verb—*I walked on this same street when I was little*. For many verbs, I add *-ed* to show that something happened in the past. Now let's look at the last sentence, where I talk about something that will happen in the future. To create the future tense, I leave the verb the same as it is and add the word *will* or *shall* in front of the verb.

> ### Modeled Writing Sample
>
> I walk to school every day, so I notice all the changes in my neighborhood. I walked on this same street when I was little, and there weren't many houses. The new homes brought new friends, but I miss the trees and fields. Someday, I hope the trees, at least, will return.

TURN AND TALK The three verb tenses are past, present, and future. Find an example of each type of verb in my writing. Explain how I formed the past and future tenses.

SUM IT UP Writers make changes to verbs depending on whether an action takes place in the present, past, or future. For regular verbs, add *-ed* to show the past tense. Add the word *will* or *shall* to the verb to show the future tense.

DAY 2   **Guided Practice**

Edit student writing on the overhead. You can use the writing sample on page 180 or allow a student volunteer to read a selection to the class and display it.

TURN AND TALK Discuss the writing's meaning and share a compliment about it. Now, think about the verbs. Do they show action in the past, present, or future? How does the writer show when the action takes place?

SUM IT UP To a class editing chart, add "For regular verbs, make the past tense by adding *-ed*. Use *will* to show the future tense."

Verb tenses show when the action in the sentence takes place. For regular verbs, show the past by adding *-ed*, and show the future by including the word *will* with the verb.

DAY 3 | **Independent Practice**

Using a writer's notebook, select a sample to model proofreading for verb tenses. Share your thinking as you look for clues that signal the use of present, past, and future tenses. Then, change the verbs accordingly. Turn the editing responsibility over to the students. Remind them that it is generally best to stick with one verb tense throughout a piece of writing.

 PEER EDIT Show your writing to your partner. Point out the verbs and talk about the tenses you used. Select one sentence and try changing the verb. Try past, present, and future. Which one fits best? How can you tell which tense to use in a piece of writing?

 SUM IT UP The tense of a verb indicates when the action of a sentence takes place. For regular verbs, add *-ed* to show past tense. To show future tense, add the helping verb *will* or *shall* to the verb.

✔ Assess the Learning

- Assess student writing for use of the three tenses. Have students point out what they do to change the verb to indicate action in the past, present, or future.

- During a writing conference, pinpoint a sentence and ask the writer why he or she chose to use a particular tense. Then, ask the writer to change the verb to a different tense and explain how to change it.

🔗 Link the Learning

- With the students, create a list of two-word sentences where the subject is in third person singular, such as *he, she, it, dog,* or *Mary,* and the verb is in the present tense. For example: *Mary walks. It howls.* Students talk about what they discover about the verbs. (They end in *s*.)

- Challenge partners to analyze a sampling of picture, chapter, and textbooks, recording the verbs on a personal chart organized by tenses. Discuss the impact of tense on the reader.

- Have students identify powerful verbs in mentor texts and write inspirational sentences on strips to post in the room. Discuss these sentences, focusing on verb tense. Challenge students to rewrite sentences putting the verbs in different tenses.

Verb Forms: Regular and Irregular

DAY 1   Model the Focus Point

Some verbs are called "regular verbs." What they have in common is that you add -*ed* to form the past tense of these verbs. I am writing about a classroom survey that was conducted a few weeks ago. It happened in the past, so I need to use a past tense verb. I add -*ed* to the verb *survey*. *Survey* is a regular verb form. Now I am writing about swimming—*Seth swimmed when he was younger*. Wait a minute, that doesn't sound right! *Swim* must be an irregular verb. The past tense of *swim* is *swam*. One of the tricky parts of irregular verbs is that they can be formed in many different ways. You have to memorize them or use a reference to help you pick the correct form. Let's look carefully at the verbs as I write.

> **Modeled Writing Sample**
>
> I surveyed my friends in class to find out their favorite sports. Matt plays football every Saturday. Seth swam when he was younger, but now he enjoys tennis. Sheila rode a bike in a competition. Today's sports will be our exercise in the future.

TURN AND TALK Find a regular verb in my writing. In what tense is that verb? How did I form that tense? Now find an irregular verb. Explain how you know it is irregular and tell how I showed the proper tense.

SUM IT UP There are regular and irregular verbs. Regular verbs form their past tense by adding -*ed*. Irregular verbs change their forms and spellings in a variety of ways.

DAY 2   Guide Practice

Place student writing on the overhead projector. Use the writing sample, page 182, or a piece from a student author. Invite a student author to read aloud to the class.

Teresa #17 — The Storm of the century Extreme storm

If you believe that the storm of the century was a blizzard, you'd be wrong. If you guessed tornado or flood, you'd still be wrong. But, if you guessed it was a combination of all three, blizzard, tornado, and flood you'd be right on.

The storm was called a nor'easter. That's when winds blow, really blow, from north-east, especially along the United States' northeast coast.

The year was 1993 when the nor'easter hit from Maine to Florida. It closed down most airports on the eastern coast. It dumped snow and caused about 50 tornadoes.

TURN AND TALK Discuss the meaning of the writing and offer a celebration to the author. Proofread the paper for past tense verbs, making sure that they are correctly formed. Classify verbs as regular or irregular.

SUM IT UP To a class editing chart, add "Add -*ed* to form the past tense of regular verbs. Check the forms of irregular verbs."

The past tense of regular verbs ends with -*ed*. Irregular verbs form past tense in other ways besides adding -*ed*.

DAY 3 | **Independent Practice**

Using a student writing folder, select a sample to model proofreading for correct forms of verbs. Share your thinking as you first identify the tense, and then check to be sure the verb is formed correctly. Use a reference that students can use as you turn the editing responsibility over to them.

 PEER EDIT Read your papers together, identifying verbs as regular or irregular. Then check how the different tenses of verbs were formed. Use a reference to check irregular verbs to be sure that they are correct. Regular verbs form their past tense by adding -*ed*. Irregular verbs change tense in other ways.

SUM IT UP Verbs can be classified as regular or irregular. Regular verbs form their past tense by adding -*ed*. Irregular verbs change their form completely or may even stay the same.

✔ Assess the Learning

- During a writing conference, have the student pinpoint both regular and irregular verbs, and contrast the two types of verbs.

- Provide a sentence from a favorite book that uses present-tense verbs. Ask students during small-group time to change the verbs to past and future tenses. Note which students need additional assistance understanding the difference between regular and irregular verbs. Provide extra support.

∞ Link the Learning

- Model this additional idea about verbs. Unless there is a compelling reason, the tenses of verbs in a sentence or paragraph should remain consistent. If you start out using past tense, stay with it. "The teacher called the parents and talks to them" is an example of a sentence that jumps from past to future tense. Students can proofread and edit for this common mistake.

- Provide students with A Guide to Common Irregular Verbs, page 158. Model and guide your students in using this resource when proofreading for verbs.

- Read Ruth Heller's *Kites Sail High: A Book About Verbs*, which honors the use of vigorous verbs and reinforces lesson cycles on tenses, regular and irregular verbs, and linking and helping verbs.

Verb Types: Linking and Helping

DAY 1   **Model the Focus Point**

We know that verbs power our sentences. Strong action verbs create vivid pictures in readers' minds. But there are other important kinds of verbs we use in our writing: linking verbs and helping verbs. These verbs do not show action, but they are still important. I'm writing a story about a silly thing I did when I was little, when I tried to teach my dog how to read. My first sentence is *Sam was my dog*. The verb is *was*. It doesn't show action; instead, it links the word *Sam* to *dog* to show that Sam was my dog. My next sentence has two verbs, *was* and *trying*. *Try* is an action verb, but adding the verb *was* shows ongoing action. It took a long time to try to teach a dog how to read! *Was* is called a helping verb in this sentence. It is paired up with another verb. When I'm finished, I'll reread to check whether I have used linking and helping verbs correctly.

> **Modeled Writing Sample**
>
> Sam <u>was</u> my dog when I was 7 years old. I <u>was trying</u> to train him. But I <u>did</u> not <u>try</u> to train him to sit, stay, or fetch. My parents <u>were</u> shocked—I wanted to teach Sam how to read! I <u>tried</u> to teach him the letters of the alphabet, but I gave up. My mom made me feel better when she told me that Sam pulled books off the shelf when I was asleep!

TURN AND TALK I used three types of verbs in my writing—action verbs, linking verbs, and helping verbs. Find an example of each type of verb.

SUM IT UP Writers use three types of verbs: action, linking, and helping verbs.

DAY 2   **Guided Practice**

Display a writing selection that includes linking and helping verbs. Use the writing sample on page 183 or a sample from your class. Invite a student author to read aloud to the class. It will be helpful to post a chart listing examples of action, linking, and helping verbs. (See Create Your Own Resources: Identifying Verb Types in the Tools section, page 156, for ideas.)

TURN AND TALK Prepare a compliment for the author as you discuss the writing. Now, think about the three types of verbs: action, linking, and helping verbs. Decide which linking or helping verbs the author used. Could he or she have included others? Where would they fit in the writing?

SUM IT UP To a class editing chart, add "Identify Three Types of Verbs: Action, Linking, or Helping."

We use different types of verbs for different purposes when writing.

Select a sample of student writing to use when you model proofreading for correct use of verb types. Refer to a chart that you have posted in the room about verb types. After sharing a think-aloud, turn the responsibility over to students to review their writing for examples of linking and helping verbs.

 PEER EDIT Share your writing with your partner. Show places where you used action, linking, and helping verbs in your writing.

 SUM IT UP Not all verbs show action. Linking verbs connect nouns with other nouns or descriptions. Helping verbs go along with main verbs to show the duration of action.

 ## Assess the Learning

- Use Create Your Own Resource: Identifying Verb Types in the Tools section, page 156, to assess student understanding. Consider having students complete the tool in small groups so you can closely observe and assess their learning.

- During writing conferences, have students explain the function of a linking verb and a helping verb by pointing out these verb types in their writing.

Link the Learning

- Read Ruth Heller's *Kites Sail High: A Book of Verbs*, stopping for a partner discussion of verbs.

- Read mentor texts with great examples of linking and helping verbs, such as George Shannon's *Tomorrow's Alphabet* and Jeanette Winter's *The Librarian of Basra*.

- Provide copies of a familiar text. Have students use scissors to cut the text apart, separating the verbs. They can then sort the verbs into action verbs, linking verbs, and phrases with helping verbs.

Single vs. Double Subjects (My mom vs. My mom she)

DAY 1 Model the Focus Point

The subject is the part of the sentence that tells who or what is doing something. As writers, we need to learn that we tell who a sentence is about one time in each sentence. I want to say: *Harriet Tubman, a conductor on the underground railroad...* I would not say, *Harriet Tubman, she was a conductor.* Harriet and "she" are the same person, so that would be telling who the sentence is about twice!!! In sentence two, I want to use *she* but I have to take a minute to be sure I am not doubling the subject. I just name the subject one time. Let's read this together and check the subject in each sentence.

> **Modeled Writing Sample**
>
> Harriet Tubman, a conductor on the underground railroad, was a very brave woman. An escaped slave herself, she spent much of her life guiding others through the night so they could be free.

TURN AND TALK What do you need to remember about the subject of the sentence? Think together about how you can remind yourselves to name the subject only once.

SUM IT UP Remember, for the subject of a sentence, use either the subject's name or a pronoun for the name, not both.

DAY 2 Guided Practice

Prepare the writing sample on page 185 from the Appendix or a selection from one of your students that includes an opportunity to talk about avoiding doubling the subject. If the author is one of your students, invite the author to read the selection to the class.

> **A Bum Rap**
> By B. B. Wolf
>
> I may be known as the Big Bad Wolf (B.B. for short). But I got a bum rap and I am here to tell you how it really went down...
>
> Slowly strolling along, my brother Al and I were out exercising his pet pig, Porkie. My brother he likes pigs a lot so he has always got a few of them wandering around in his yard for company. As we meandered along minding our own business, this really bossy mama pig comes raging up and demands that we come and help her kids. She says they are trapped in their house and need someone to help get them out.
>
> Quickly, me and my brother grabbed Porkie and went racing to the pigs' house. Just like that bossy mama said, there were three pig faces in the window looking scared as can be and the door was stuck tight.
>
> With a huge puff of shared wolf-power my brother and I huffed and we puffed and we blew as hard as we could. Sure enough that house blew down and there sat three confused looking little pigs.
>
> You can imagine how surprised we were when the police came roaring up and threw Al and me in jail.

TURN AND TALK Writers, talk about the meaning of the writing. Then offer a specific compliment about something the writer did well. Go back and reread each sentence and identify the subject. Then, check to see if the author doubled up on the subject by saying, for example, *The earth's people, they...*

SUM IT UP Remember, for the subject of a sentence, use either the subject's name or a pronoun for the name, not both.

Guide writers in selecting a different piece of writing, then show how you proofread and edit for doubling up on the subject. Give them a few minutes to put on their editors' caps to check their own writing.

 PEER EDIT Take turns pointing out the subject of each of your sentences. Together, carefully proofread each paper for any double subjects.

 SUM IT UP Remember, for the subject of a sentence, use either the subject's name or a pronoun for the name, not both.

✔ Assess the Learning

- Observe editors at work, and make note of which students are still doubling up subjects in the sentences.

- During small-group reading instruction, have readers identify the subjects of sentences and note whether the author used a noun or a pronoun in each sentence.

∞ Link the Learning

- During writer's workshop, remind students to check their subjects to be sure they didn't double up. Help writers apply what they know as they craft writing selections.

- Teach a cycle about compound subjects. Demonstrate how compound subjects such as Mom and Dad are correct, while double subjects such as "My mom, she . . ." are incorrect.

- Have each student identify a sentence from a favorite book that names a person. Discuss why the author selected a noun vs. a pronoun and speculate about why the author structured the sentence as he or she did. Have students find any examples when the author doubled the subject by using both the person's name and a pronoun.

Singular Subject-Verb Agreement

DAY 1 Model the Focus Point

We know that when we write a sentence, we need to have a subject and a verb. Once the sentence has both parts, we need to be sure that those parts agree with each other. I am writing about Snooty, a manatee in captivity, and comparing him to a manatee that lives in the wild. Because I am writing about one manatee, I need to use verbs that agree with singular subjects—singular means "one." My first sentence already sounds off—*Snooty, a manatee, live in the South Florida Museum.* What's missing from the verb? The verb needs to end with the letter *s. Snooty lives in Florida*—that sounds better, because my singular subject has a singular verb. Let's think about the verb *swim.* If I am talking about more than one manatee, I would use *swim* in this sentence, but I am only writing about one animal, so I'll add an *s* to the end of the verb.

> **Modeled Writing Sample**
>
> Snooty, a manatee, live in a South Florida museum. He was born in 1948, making him the oldest manatee in captivity. A wild manatee swim in warm coastal waters rather than a museum. This animal eats over 60 different species of plants, up to 9 percent of its body weight each day.

TURN AND TALK All the subjects are singular in my writing. I'd like you to pick out the verbs that agree with these singular subjects. Singular verbs that you often see include *is, was, has,* and action verbs that end with *s.* Add another sentence about a single manatee. Use a singular verb!

SUM IT UP If you write about a singular subject, you need to use a singular verb, such as *is, was, has,* or an action verb that ends with an *s.*

DAY 2 Guided Practice

Place student writing on the overhead projector. Use the writing sample on page 181, or a sample from your class that includes mostly singular subjects and verbs. If the author is one of your students, invite the author to read the selection to the class.

TURN AND TALK Note: Partners will need a blank piece of paper and a pencil.

First, talk over the meaning of the selection and share a compliment about the writing. Now, make a T-chart and label the columns *subject* and *verb.* Reread the writing and record the subject and verb from each sentence. Put a star near any singular nouns in the chart. Be sure the verbs match.

SUM IT UP To a class editing chart, add "Singular subjects need singular verbs."

Remember, your subject and verb need to agree. When you have a singular subject, you need to have a singular verb as well.

DAY 3 | Independent Practice

Model how to look for subject-verb agreement in a piece of writing that you select from a writing folder. Allow writers a few minutes to identify singular subjects in their papers and make sure that the verbs agree. Remind them that singular verbs include *is*, *was*, *has*, and action verbs that end with *s*.

 PEER EDIT Partners, work together to find singular subjects and verbs. What verbs did you find? Share the sentences with singular subjects and correctly used verbs.

 SUM IT UP Subjects and verbs need to agree. A singular subject requires a singular verb, such as *is*, *has*, *was*, or an action verb that ends with *s*.

✔ Assess the Learning

- Keep track of students who make subjects and verbs agree in their writing. Using your class record-keeping grid, note the students whose verbs and subjects agree and those who need extra support.

- During writing conferences or small-group reading sessions, ask students to point out singular subjects and verbs. What do they notice about the verbs?

∞ Link the Learning

- Encourage students to find examples of singular subjects and verbs in agreement in content-area texts, such as science lab procedures, math story problems, and so on.

- Create index cards with singular nouns, corresponding plural nouns, and singular verbs, one word to each card. Students can work in small groups to match singular nouns with verbs that agree.

- Students identify powerful singular verbs in mentor texts or in their own writing. Have them add verbs to a word wall for inspiration. Encourage students to explain what makes these verbs so powerful and precise—what images do these verbs create?

Plural Subject-Verb Agreement

DAY 1   Model the Focus Point

Remember the writing we did about the manatee named Snooty? Snooty was just one manatee. Today I am going to write about many manatees. A noun that refers to more than one is a plural noun. Just like singular nouns, plural nouns need to agree with their subjects. Listen to my first sentence—*Manatees swims in warm waters*. I used *swims* with a single manatee, but I need to take the *-s* off the end of the verb when the noun is plural. Let's try again. *Manatees swim...* Yes, that sounds much better! If I were talking about one manatee, I could say *This animal munches*; but, since I am talking about more than one animal, I need to remove the *-es* from the verb to make *munch*. I know with singular nouns, I can use the verb *has*. But that doesn't sound right here—*They have no natural enemies*. I need to use the plural form, *have*, with the pronoun *they*.

> ### Modeled Writing Sample
>
> Manatees swims in warm waters off the coast of Florida. These animals munch over 60 different species of plants, up to 9 percent of their body weight each day. They have no natural enemies, but they are still in danger. Manatees often glide too close to boats, where they can be injured by the motor.

TURN AND TALK Plural subjects and plural verbs are different from singular ones. What have you noticed about plural verbs? List some plural verbs from my writing as well as a few others that you know.

SUM IT UP When writing about two or more people, places, or things, write their names or the word *they* in the subject. The verbs you use might include *are*, *were*, *have*, or action verbs that do not have an *-s* or *-es* added to them.

DAY 2   Guided Practice

Place student writing on the overhead projector. Use the writing sample on page 186, or a sample from your class that includes plural subjects and verbs. If the author is one of your students, invite the author to read the selection to the class.

> ### Proper Tooth Care...A MUST!!!
> By David S. and Carolyn H.
>
> Do you want false teeth when you get old? Do you want root canals when your not even old? If you don't start taking better care of your teeth these could be your future!
>
> Kids' teeth should be in much better shape than they are. We interviewed kindergartens through fifth graders and your mouth would fall open and hit the ground if you heard what we heard!!
>
> Four out of every five kids went to bed WITHOUT brushing their teeth at least one night every week. Just think. All those germs spending a 10 hour recess in your mouth just wrecking your teeths' chance for a good healthy life.
>
> Even MORE alarming (we only checked with the 4th and 5th graders on this question) only one in 10 kids flossed! The dentists' opinion is that this is extremely important to get rid of plaque, which causes tooth decay too.
>
> We didn't even ask kids if they were eating junk food, we just watched and almost everybody did. We know that we should eat better, more fruits, vegetables, and less candy. This will help our teeth.

TURN AND TALK Talk about the text's meaning and offer a compliment to the writer. Read the selection and identify plural verbs. Discuss with your partner how the verbs would change if you used singular subjects instead of plural ones.

SUM IT UP To a class editing chart, add "Plural subjects need plural verbs."

Remember, subjects and verbs have to agree. If you have a plural subject, you need to use a corresponding plural verb.

Look through a writing folder to locate a piece of writing with plural subjects. Show your students how you proofread for agreement with plural subjects and plural verbs. Then, turn the editing process over to students so they can be sure that plural subjects and their verbs agree.

 PEER EDIT Proofread together. Point out the plural subjects and read the verbs to see if they agree. How can you fix verbs that do not agree with their plural subjects?

 SUM IT UP Subjects and verbs in sentences need to agree. Plural subjects need plural verbs.

✔ Assess the Learning

- Observe editors at work, using a class record-keeping grid to check off the students who correctly make plural subjects and verbs agree.

- Confer with readers during independent reading time and have them identify singular and plural subjects and verbs in their selections. They can compare and contrast singular and plural verbs.

🔗 Link the Learning

- Give students wipe-off boards. Say a verb. Students write the verb and identify whether it is a singular or plural verb. Then they can write a suitable subject for the verb. Partners can quickly check each other's work for accuracy.

- Write sentences with both singular subjects and plural subjects on sentence strips. Cut the sentences, separating the subjects from the verbs. Students can work in teams to put suitable sentences together. As students gain proficiency, they can create sentences and cut them apart for other groups to assemble.

- Have students reread a section from their independent reading book, selecting two sentences with plural subjects and verbs. Have them record the sentences in their writers' notebooks and then share the plural subjects and corresponding verbs with a partner.

Pronoun Order: Person's Name and Then *I*, Not *Me*

DAY 1 | Model the Focus Point

I am writing a story about a memory of my grandpa. When I write about another person and I am in the story, too, I usually need to put the other person's name first and follow with *I* rather than *me*. So I start the story with *My grandpa and I*, not *my grandpa and me*. In sentence two, I want to tell that I got to play a duet with my sister. I need to say, *my sister\ and I...* In sentence three, I am listing three people, my grandpa, my sister and me. I need to follow the rule and list everyone else first, so I will say, *Grandpa, my sister, and I...* This pattern works even for a list of people.

Modeled Writing Sample

My grandfather and I spent many special hours with our fingers dancing over the keyboard of his piano. With Grandpa as coach, my sister and I even played a duet. Grandpa, my sister, and I made amazing music—and wonderful memories!

TURN AND TALK Find a place in the writing where I used a subject and a pronoun in the right order. Find a place where I avoided using a double subject. Explain those two rules to your partner.

SUM IT UP In general, write the other person's name first, followed by *I* and not by *me*.

DAY 2 | Guided Practice

Display the writing sample, "A Bum Rap," on page 185, or a student sample that needs a second look at subject noun-pronoun order. Invite student authors to read their work.

TURN AND TALK Share one thing you particularly like about this writing. Then proofread. Did the author remember to put the other person's name before the pronoun? Which pronoun did he or she use to refer to himself or herself? What suggestions can you offer?

A Bum Rap
By B. B. Wolf

I may be known as the Big Bad Wolf (B.B. for short). But I got a bum rap and I am here to tell you how it really went down...

Slowly strolling along, my brother Al and I were out exercising his pet pig, Porkie. My brother he likes pigs a lot so he has always got a few of them wandering around in his yard for company. As we meandered along minding our own business, this really bossy mama pig comes raging up and demands that we come and help her kids. She says they are trapped in their house and need someone to help get them out.

Quickly, me and my brother grabbed Porkie and went racing to the pigs' house. Just like that bossy mama said, there were three pig faces in the window looking scared as can be and the door was stuck tight.

With a huge puff of shared wolf-power my brother and I we huffed and we puffed and we blew as hard as we could. Sure enough that house blew down and there sat three confused looking little pigs.

You can imagine how surprised we were when the police came roaring up and threw Al and me in jail.

SUM IT UP To a class editing chart, add "In a compound subject, write other person's name first, and then I."

Remember to write the other person's name first, then write *I* when you are in the story, too.

DAY 3 | **Independent Practice**

Have partners practice proofreading and editing subjective noun-pronoun order with you before turning to their own writing folders to review their work for noun-pronoun order.

 PEER EDIT Use a sticky note to mark places where you wrote about yourself and someone else. Go back and check to be sure that you put the other person's name first in each instance.

 SUM IT UP In writing and speaking, we put another person's name before our own name.

✓ **Assess the Learning**

- Gather the writing samples tabbed by students for the peer editing in this cycle and assess understanding of noun-pronoun order.

- As your students work, note which of them are still having difficulty using the "___ and I" pattern rather than "I and ____" or "me and _____" in compound subjects.

∞ **Link the Learning**

- Expand the lesson by applying noun-pronoun order to sentences with three or more subjects, such as "Katie, Shanin, Christy, and I…" Have students create sentences of their own to save in their writer's notebooks or to display on sentence strips.

- Have students review their independent reading selections for examples of noun-pronoun order in a mentor book. Post their findings and cite the sources.

- Give students plentiful opportunities to use correct noun-pronoun order in daily conversation. Example: *Amanda and I would like to go to the library during recess. Julio and I would be happy to clean off the boards for you today. Mr. Smith and I were discussing our next buddy reading time and decided that…*

Pronouns and Their Antecedents

DAY 1 · Model the Focus Point

One of our goals as writers is to be sure that readers are not confused by our writing. It sounds simple enough, but sometimes it's tricky. When we use pronouns like *he*, *she*, *it*, *we*, or *they* in our writing, it's important to check and be sure our readers know who or what we are describing. I am writing a poem about night. I start with the line *She cushions stars*. I have a pronoun, *she*. But it's not clear at all what I am referring to! The noun that I refer to is called an *antecedent*. This pronoun does not have a clear antecedent. I need to add a line before this one—*Night is a velvet pillow*. Now the antecedent is clear. *She* refers to *night*. Let's look at this line of the poem: *He says, "You must go. It is my time to stay."* There are two pronouns here, *he* and *you*. Do these pronouns have clear antecedents? Let's check!

> **Modeled Writing Sample**
>
> Shadow and Light
>
> Night is a velvet pillow
> She cushions stars
> Her darkness soothes the Earth
>
> The rising sun greets the night
> He says, "You must go. This is my time."
> His light nudges her aside.

TURN AND TALK Think together. Identify all the pronouns I used. Then identify the antecedent for each pronoun.

SUM IT UP Pronouns must clearly refer to something. We call that something an antecedent.

DAY 2 · Guided Practice

Display student writing on the overhead projector. Use the writing sample on page 188 or a selection by a student author. Invite the student author to read aloud to the class.

> **A Harry Potter Book Review by Carlos M.**
>
> My favorite author is JK Rowling. Everyone knows she has written the Harry Potter books. She teaches us lessons about life and entertains us. I think she does a good job of developing her characters. Even Harry isn't perfect all the time. I've had some of his problems with friends and schoolwork.
>
> I am reading the fifth book, Order Of The Phoenix. If I was JK, I would have written these chapter titles:" The Order Begins"," Kids on a Mission","Lessons Learned", and " Fighting for Justice". I won't tell you which chapters they go with. You'll need to read the book and make a guess. Then will I let you know!
>
> Anyone want to have a Harry Potter book club? Let me know. I love to talk about Harry!

TURN AND TALK Writers, talk about the meaning of the writing. Offer a specific compliment to the author, then reread each sentence, stopping to decide if you always know to whom the pronoun is referring. If you aren't certain, then double check for the noun's name, the antecedent.

SUM IT UP To a class editing chart, add "Pronouns need clear antecedents."

Whenever you use a pronoun in your writing, check to be sure that it has a clear antecedent, or a noun or nouns to which the pronoun refers.

Model thumbing through a writing folder to select a piece of writing with pronouns. Proofread and edit, letting students see your thinking about pronouns and their antecedents. Allow time for students to take over editing where you leave off.

 PEER EDIT Partners, take turns reading your writing and pointing out the pronouns you used. Identify the antecedents. Are there any pronouns for which the antecedents are unclear? If so, add the antecedent.

 SUM IT UP A pronoun takes the place of a noun, but that pronoun needs a clear antecedent. You don't want readers to be confused about the pronouns you use in your writing.

 ## Assess the Learning

- Provide sentences with pronouns, such as "I left it right here, but now it's gone" and "Their pencils scribbling furiously, they finished their test with only a few minutes to spare." Have students cut the sentences apart so that they can omit one of the pronouns to replace it with a noun.

- As you confer with individuals during writing conferences, ask them to identify a pronoun and point out its antecedent. Assist those who need extra help.

Link the Learning

- Read aloud a mentor text, deliberately replacing all the names with pronouns. Ask students to discuss what happens when only pronouns are used in sentences.

- Read aloud another favorite book, replacing the pronouns with their antecedents. Students will probably find the writing boring and repetitive without pronouns. Have students orally "rewrite" some of your boring sentences.

- Students can select writing from their folders and check to be sure that there is a balance between nouns and pronouns. Encourage them to rewrite for clarity and variety.

- Use the assessment tool Identifying Pronouns and Their Antecedents, on page 171. Have students fill in the blanks with nouns rather than pronouns and discuss the impact on the text.

Pronouns: Possessive

DAY 1 | Model the Focus Point

Possessive pronouns do two things at once. They take the place of a noun, and they show ownership. When you use possessive pronouns, you don't use an apostrophe as you do with possessive nouns. I am writing about an argument between two brothers over their socks. Let's read this sentence: *I thought those socks were my socks*. The sentence sounds kind of dull with the word *socks* in it twice. I want to write something that flows better. How about this? *I thought those socks were mine*. The word *mine* is a possessive pronoun. It replaces the whole phrase *my socks*. In the next sentence, how can I replace the phrase *his socks*? I can say, *my brother was certain they were his*.

> **Modeled Writing Sample**
>
> My brother and I had an argument every morning, an argument over socks. Every time I picked up a pair, I thought those socks were *mine*. But my brother was certain they were *his*. Finally, my mom bought us bags of white socks that all match. Now the socks are *ours*.

TURN AND TALK Writers, find all the possessive pronouns. What phrases did each of those possessive pronouns replace? How did using possessive pronouns make my writing flow more smoothly?

SUM IT UP Possessive pronouns show ownership and often take the place of longer phrases. You don't use an apostrophe with possessive pronouns. Possessive pronouns include *mine, ours, his, hers, theirs,* and *yours*.

DAY 2 | Guided Practice

Use the writing sample on page 184, or a sample from your class that includes possessive pronouns, as a guided practice piece on the overhead. If the author is one of your students, he or she might want to read it to the class.

TURN AND TALK Discuss the meaning of the piece and share a compliment about the writing. Now, think together about how the author showed ownership. Identify the possessive pronouns and double check to be sure that they do not include apostrophes.

SUM IT UP To a class editing chart, add "Possessive pronouns show ownership."

Writers can use possessive pronouns to take the place of possessive phrases.

> Cecelia
>
> Yours, Mine, and Ours
>
> My sister and me share a bedroom. Sometimes its great to have a roommate and other times its horendous. We came up with a way to stop our fighting. Its called "Yours, mine, and Ours". Our parents bought us our own dressers. Now we have our own sides of the room too. We share a work table, but we each have our own box of supplys.
>
> Now we just need to keep our little brother out but thats easier said then done !!

Select a writing sample from a writing folder that includes possessive pronouns. Model your thinking as you proofread for correct use of possessive pronouns. Have students continue the process.

 PEER EDIT First, discuss the two things that possessive pronouns do for a writer. (They show ownership and replace a noun.) **Take turns looking at each other's writing. Partners, identify possessive pronouns in your partner's writing.**

 SUM IT UP To show ownership and avoid repeating nouns and possessive noun phrases, you can use possessive pronouns, such as *his, ours, mine, yours, hers,* and *theirs*.

 ## ✔ Assess the Learning

- Confer with individuals during writing conferences and assess how well they are using possessive pronouns. Ask the student to identify the possessive pronoun and tell the word or phrase it replaces.

- Ask students to write a list of possessive pronouns and indicate whether they are singular or plural.

🔗 Link the Learning

- Students can create and post a chart of possessive pronouns to use as a reference in the classroom.

	Writing about/to	Use possessive pronoun
1st person	yourself	mine
	yourself & someone else	ours
2nd person	you	yours
3rd person	one female	hers
	one male	his
	more than one	theirs

- Hold up or describe an item in the classroom and ask a question that volunteers can answer with possessive pronouns. Examples: *Whose pencil is this? That pencil is his. Whose desks are these? These desks are ours.* Students may enjoy devising questions to ask classmates.

- Have students review a familiar text and keep track of the number of times they find possessive pronouns in a five-minute reading. Provide an opportunity for them to share their findings.

Nouns and Pronouns: Subjective and Objective Cases

Model the Focus Point

Note: There are many ways to teach the subjective and objective cases. This lesson is one example. The following chart is an important reference.

Subjective Case Pronouns (Used in the subject or after a linking verb)	Objective Case Pronouns (Used in the predicate as an object of an action verb or after a preposition)
I, you, he, she, it, we, they, who	*me, you, him, her, it, us, them, whom*

Modeled Writing Sample

The Florida manatee is an aquatic relative of the elephant. They are water-dwelling mammals whose flippers help them steer through shallow water.

Writers, did you know that the form of the pronoun you use depends on how it is used in the sentence? If you replace the subject of a sentence with a pronoun, you usually select a pronoun from the subjective-case pronoun list. If the pronoun replaces a noun in the predicate or after a preposition, you usually use the objective case. For my second sentence, I want to say *manatees are water animals*. I am replacing *manatee*, the subject, with a pronoun. Let's look at the chart and decide, would I select *they* or *them*? As I end this sentence and work on the predicate, I need another pronoun for *manatees*. Going to the chart again, I have to think, should it be *flippers help them* or *flippers help they*? See how this chart can help me make good choices?

 TURN AND TALK Think together about the pronouns I selected. What helped me decide which pronouns to use? How might this chart help you?

SUM IT UP Subjective pronouns are often used in the subject of a sentence or in the predicate after a linking verb. Objective pronouns often follow an action verb or a preposition.

Guided Practice

Place a piece of student writing on the overhead projector. Use the writing sample on page 186 or a sample from your class that includes pronouns. If the author is one of your students, invite the author to read the selection to the class.

 TURN AND TALK What celebration can you offer the writer? Discuss the meaning of the text, then look for subjective and objective case pronouns. Use the chart to consider the pronouns the writer selected. Do you have any suggestions?

**A True American Hero
The Story of Rosa Parks**

She wasn't a tall woman or a loud woman. She wasn't a woman who made a scene. She was a tired woman, riding a bus, heading home after a long days work.

As the bus filled up, Rosa Parks sat quietly, until the bus drive told her that she needed to give up her seat to a white man. He expected this quiet black woman to follow his order, figuring that no black person would face jail just for a bus seat. He was wrong.

Mrs. Parks decided to stand up for her rights by remaining seated. She was arrested and went to trial. But this quiet lady, Dr. Martin Luther King, and thousands of others changed America forever. They did it without violence. They had a dream and followed it. Mrs. Rosa Parks is a TRUE American hero. I thank you.

SUM IT UP To a class editing chart, add "Usually, writers use subjective pronouns when they are the subject or when they follow a linking verb and name or rename the subject. We use objective pronouns after an action verb or a preposition."

Writers, tools such as our chart of subjective and objective pronouns can help us make good choices about the pronouns in our writing. Be sure to wonder if the pronoun is going into the subject of a sentence or if it will follow an action verb or a preposition.

DAY 3 Independent Practice

From a writing folder, select writing that includes pronouns. Then, using the posted pronouns, explain your thinking as you proofread for proper placement of subjective and objective pronouns. Turn the task over to the students as they review their own writing folders for subjective and objective pronouns.

 PEER EDIT Put a sticky note next to any pronoun in the writing and discuss whether those pronouns are the subject or object in the sentences. Then use the chart to edit, making sure pronouns are placed properly in sentences.

 SUM IT UP *I, we, you, he, she, it*, and *they* are subjective pronouns and are used to take the place of the subject of a sentence. *Me, us, you, her, him, it*, and *them* are objective pronouns, which are used in the predicate of a sentence or after a preposition.

✔ Assess the Learning

- Have students identify subjective and objective case pronouns in a mentor text. Encourage them to explain how they know which case is appropriate for a particular sentence.

- As you observe writers at work, use a class record-keeping grid to make note of their progress with subjective and objective case pronouns. Provide extra support for students who still need assistance. Refer them to the chart.

Link the Learning

- Type sentences that include pronouns from familiar mentor books in large letters. Then, have partners cut the sentences apart, separating subjects and predicates. Once sentences are cut up, have partners identify the pronouns as subjective or objective depending on their function in the sentence.

- Write sentences on strips and distribute to pairs. Make sure to include a mix of singular and plural nouns as both the subject and object of the sentences. Partners can replace the nouns in the sentences with pronouns.

- Have students select a sentence that includes pronouns from a favorite book then prepare to explain to a partner about the choices the author made with subjective and objective pronouns.

Adjectives to Lift Descriptions

DAY 1   Model the Focus Point

Note: Read aloud from a mentor text that includes vivid adjectives, deliberately leaving out the adjectives. (Suggestion: *Amos and Boris* by William Steig) Then, read it again, with the adjectives in place.

How were my two readings different? What happened to the text when those amazing adjectives were removed? Adding strong adjectives—words that are used to describe nouns and pronouns—helps create vivid pictures in our readers' minds as they read. One of my favorite adjectives is *stellar*. It means almost perfect! I am going to write some stellar adjectives in my writer's notebook. I will select adjectives from this mentor to get me started. Think together, which words create a strong impression in your mind? Which ones are "stellar?"

Modeled Writing Sample		
stellar	essential	envious
cherished	grumpy	gloomy
fretful	bewildering	gleeful
startled	bulbous	glistening
flowing	gigantic	sparkling
embarrassed	short-cropped	

TURN AND TALK Take a look at my list of adjectives. Which of these would you include on a list of your own? Add them to your writer's notebook. Then share a few other stellar adjectives with your partner.

SUM IT UP Adjectives are words that describe nouns and pronouns. You can improve your writing by using specific and sparkling adjectives rather than tired ones, like *nice* or *big*.

DAY 2   Guided Practice

Display the writing sample on page 189 or a sample from a student author that includes opportunities to use rich adjectives. If the author is one of your students, invite him or her to read the selection to the class.

The Heart

With unrelenting consistency, the muscles of the heart squeeze together. These contractions of the heart are so powerful they could send a jet of water six feet high into the air. Each time the muscles contract, blood surges through the chambers of the heart gathering speed, pulsing with power. As the blood pushes out of the left ventricle of the heart, it smashes with great force into the aorta, the blood vessel that directs blood away from the heart and toward the rest of the body. Deep and fast, blood streams into ever-smaller tunnels. Shivery and quick, blood travels into veins and capillaries delivering oxygen and nutrients to needy cells.

TURN AND TALK Discuss the meaning of the piece as you craft a compliment for the writer. Then talk about the adjectives. Which adjectives really sparkled for you? What pictures did those adjectives create in your mind? Think of a place where an adjective could be replaced with one that is even more precise and vivid. Are there any places where an adjective could be added?

SUM IT UP To a class editing chart, add "Choose stellar adjectives!"
Carefully craft your sentences to include adjectives that create vivid descriptions that help readers visualize.

DAY 3 | **Independent Practice**

Have writers review their writer's notebooks or a sample from their writing folders that they want to enrich with stellar adjectives. Post the stellar adjectives from your modeled writing for inspiration. Give writers time to reread, add or replace adjectives, and get ready to share with partners.

 PEER EDIT Discuss adjectives in your writing. Evaluate the adjectives, suggesting additional or different ones that would ratchet up the writing to a new level. Look in your writer's notebook at the stellar adjectives you are collecting for inspiration.

SUM IT UP Well-chosen adjectives are like jewels. They make writing sparkle!

✔ Assess the Learning

- Analyze students' writing for vivid adjectives. Using a class record-keeping grid, track writers who take risks with vivid adjectives and those who may benefit from more coaching.

- During independent reading, confer with individuals to assess their ability to recognize adjectives and to choose vivid examples. Encourage students to continue to record favorite adjectives for inspiration and to use in their writing.

∞ Link the Learning

- Highlight picture books and other mentor texts with exquisite language, particularly powerful adjectives. Help students notice that exquisite adjectives are not just strings of descriptors. They are carefully painted images. Examples to consider: *A Drop of Water* by Walter Wick, *Owl Moon* by Jane Yolen, *Under the Quilt of Night* by Deborah Hopkinson, *Dogteam* by Gary Paulsen, *Annie and the Old One* by Miska Miles.

- Conduct a scavenger hunt for terrific adjectives. Have partners search for and record the best examples they can find. Students can record sentences on strips and post them for inspiration or collect them in their writer's notebooks for later reference.

- Keep a chart of tantalizing words from read-alouds and encourage students to record their favorites as well. Model making a conscious effort to use words from the chart in writing and in daily conversation.

- Invite students to create a visual image in words, using stellar adjectives and powerful verbs to show the scene rather than tell about it. Telling sentences: *The room was messy and the teenager was really mad.* Beginning of a showing paragraph: *Slamming the door, the furious teenager threw himself between the piles of dirty clothes, randomly tossed schoolwork, and a plate of food just beginning to mold. A picture of churning frustration, he slammed his fist into the pillow and wished he could start the day again.*

Adjectives: Comparative and Superlative Forms

DAY 1 **Model the Focus Point**

I am going to hold three objects—listen to me as I describe them. *This globe is heavy. The book is heavier than the globe. This thick dictionary is the heaviest of all.* Did you notice how I described them? I added *-er* to an adjective to compare two things. The adjective, *heavier*, is in the comparative form. When I compare more than two, I add *-est* to the adjective. The adjective, *heaviest*, is in the superlative form. Now listen as I describe the items again. *A globe is useful in my writing. To me, this book is more useful than the globe. But the dictionary is the most useful tool of all.* I wouldn't say that a book is *usefuller!* So I use *more* and *most* to make my comparisons. Watch as I use comparatives and superlatives in my writing.

> **Modeled Writing Sample**
>
> Today's pizza was the greatest lunch ever! Our school lunches are usually tasty, but this lunch was tastier than ever and one of the most delicious meals we've ever had. The addition of a whole wheat crust and veggies also made this one of the healthiest lunches we've been served here.

 TURN AND TALK What did you notice about my comparisons? Write down the comparison words I used in this writing and classify them as comparative or superlative. Talk about forming comparatives and superlatives. What do you need to remember?

SUM IT UP We can compare nouns or pronouns using *-er*, *-est*, *more*, and *most*. Multisyllable words often need *more* and *most* or *less* and *least* for their comparative and superlative forms.

DAY 2 **Guided Practice**

Display this writing sample from the Appendix, page 188, or one from a student author in your class. If the author is a student, invite him or her to read aloud to the class.

> **A Harry Potter Book Review by Carlos M.**
>
> My favorite author is JK Rowling. Everyone knows she has written the Harry Potter books. She teaches us lessons about life and entertains us. I think she does a good job of developing her characters. Even Harry isn't perfect all the time. I've had some of his problems with friends and schoolwork.
>
> I am reading the fifth book, Order Of The Phoenix. If I was JK, I would have written these chapter titles: "The Order Begins", "Kids on a Mission", "Lessons Learned", and "Fighting for Justice". I won't tell you which chapters they go with. You'll need to read the book and make a guess. Then will I let you know!
>
> Anyone want to have a Harry Potter book club? Let me know. I love to talk about Harry!

TURN AND TALK Discuss the meaning of the writing and offer a compliment to the author. Then reread the selection with the idea of including interesting comparisons using *-er*, *-est*, *more*, and *most*, *less* and *least*.

SUM IT UP To a class editing chart, add "Show comparisons with *–er*, *–est*, *more*, and *most*."

Comparative adjectives compare two objects while superlative adjectives compare more than two. With short adjectives, you can add *-er* or *-est*. For longer adjectives, you may need to use *more* and *most/less* and *least* to make comparisons.

DAY 3 | **Independent Practice**

Share your thinking as you reread an existing piece of writing to insert comparisons. Allow time for writers to rethink and insert comparisons that make the writing more colorful and descriptive.

 PEER EDIT Work together to find pieces in your writing folders where you can add comparative and superlative adjectives. Check to be sure that you use *-er* and *more* when comparing two objects and *-est* and *most* when comparing more than two.

 SUM IT UP Use comparative and superlative adjectives to make your writing colorful and specific. Form words with *-er* or *-est*, or add *more* and *most* as modifiers.

✅ Assess the Learning

- Confer with writers and ask them to use a variety of comparative forms to compare real things in the classroom. Identify those who can compare using regular forms and those who are ready for irregular or special comparatives.

- Have students create a page in their writer's notebook where they collect and save comparatives they find in their reading and in their own writing. Gather the notebooks and assess the comparatives they have collected.

Link the Learning

- To spark students' imagination, share Judi Barrett's use of superlatives in *Things That Are the Most in the World*. Challenge partners to write their own short stories using comparative or superlative adjectives.

- Teach terms associated with these forms: comparatives compare two nouns/pronouns; superlatives compare three or more nouns/pronouns.

- Some adjectives use completely different words to show comparison. Provide your students with the opportunity to compare using a broad range of language forms.

	Comparative	Superlative
Bad	worse	worst
Good	better	best
Many	more	most

- Point out spelling changes that occur in some comparatives, such as: consonant-*y* patterns, change the *y* to *i* and add the ending (*funny, funnier, funniest; happy, happier, happiest*). Have students conduct a scavenger hunt for regular comparatives and those that require a special rule.

Adverbs: Comparative and Superlative Forms

DAY 1 **Model the Focus Point**

Adverbs follow the same rules for comparison as adjectives. To create the comparative and superlative forms, we add an *er* or *est* to one-syllable adverbs (*fast, faster, fastest*) and add the words *more* or *less* before adverbs with two or more syllables (*carefully, more carefully, most carefully*). I am writing about training for a track meet. I trained harder for the big race than I had before, so I use a comparative adverb. I add -*er* to the adverb *hard*. Listen to my next sentence—*I wanted to run swiftlier so that I could qualify for the state meet.* Wait a minute—that doesn't sound correct. To form the comparative form of an adjective with two syllables, I need to use the word *more* in front of the adverb. When I compare two or more actions in the next sentence, I use the word *most*.

> ### Modeled Writing Sample
>
> I trained harder before the big race. I wanted to run more swiftly so that I could qualify for the state meet. On the big day, I approached the starting gate the most seriously I ever had. I glanced at my competitors, realizing that I would have to run my fastest. I turned in my best performance, and I qualified for state. My hard work had paid off!

 TURN AND TALK With your partner, find both a comparative and a superlative adverb. Explain the rules I followed for forming them.

 SUM IT UP Comparative adverbs compare two actions while superlative adverbs compare more than two. Add *er* and *est* to form comparative and superlative forms of adverbs with one syllable. In general, use *more* and *most* for adverbs with two or more syllables.

DAY 2 **Guided Practice**

Place student writing on the overhead projector. Use the writing sample on page 187 or a selection from your class. If the author is one of your students, invite the author to read the selection aloud.

 TURN AND TALK Discuss the meaning of the writing and offer a compliment to the author. Proofread the paper for adverbs that compare. Suggest a place where a comparative or superlative adverb could make the writing even stronger.

 SUM IT UP To a class editing chart, add "To compare adverbs, use –*er*, –*est*, *more* and *most*, *less* and *least*"

Remember, use -*er* and -*est* to form comparative and superlative forms of one-syllable adverbs. For adverbs of two or more syllables, use *more* and *most*, *less* and *least*.

Show writers how to look through writing folders to find writing with adverbs that compare. Let your students see your thinking as you proofread for or add comparative or superlative adverbs, then turn the task over to students.

 PEER EDIT Take turns reading your writing and pointing out adverbs that compare. Find places to add new comparing adverbs. Discuss the rules you followed for writing comparative and superlative adverbs.

 SUM IT UP Remember, comparative adverbs compare two actions, while superlative adverbs compare more than two. Add -*er* and -*est* to form comparative and superlative forms of adverbs with one syllable. In general, use *more* and *most*, *less* and *least* for adverbs with two or more syllables.

✅ Assess the Learning

- Give students a few adverbs of one or more syllables. Students provide examples of comparative and superlative adverbs. Note students who need additional instruction individually or in small groups.

- Ask students to write out the rules for adverb forms. Analyze the level of understanding.

⚭ Link the Learning

- Introduce special adverb forms. Some adverbs use different words to compare, such as *well*, *better*, *best*.

Positive	Comparative	Superlative
much	more	most
little	less	least
well	better	best
badly	worse	worst

- Using the adverb list created in Adverbs and Adverb Phrases, add columns for comparing adverb forms. With the students, record examples of adverbs that compare.

- Give special attention to:
  - *Good* is always an adjective. *Well* can be either an adjective or adverb.
  - *Bad* is always an adjective. *Badly* is an adverb.
  - *Real* is the adjective. *Really* is the adverb.

- Teach hyperbole, a literary device of deliberate exaggeration. Comparative and superlative adverbs, in addition to similes and metaphors, are tools of hyperbole. You will find great examples in books such as *Piggy Pie* by Margie Palatini, *Library Lil* by Steven Kellogg, *The Bunyans* by Audrey Wood, and *Golem* by David Wisnewski.

Cycles for Moving Forward With Spelling

It has been well proven that spelling is developmental, that it goes hand in hand with print knowledge in reading and in writing. In addition to print knowledge, children need to have spelling strategies that address the challenges of crafting meaningful writing with spelling that can be read by others. When writers approach spelling tasks strategically, they gain a sense of when to rely on their own knowledge of spelling patterns and when to use the word wall or a dictionary. Because strategic spellers know how to navigate their work as word-builders, they pay attention to the way words look and notice patterns in words. Strategic spellers have a distinct sense of *spelling consciousness* that guides them in their writing.

Spelling Strategies Self-Assessment

Writer_____ Date _____

During drafting, when I come to a word I am not sure of, I usually _____

or _____. During editing, I would follow up on the word by _____

_____ or _____.

Mark the strategies you use: (Put a star next to the ones you use the most)

❏ Stretch words out slowly and listen to sounds

❏ Draw a line under words I am not sure of during drafting or write sp.

❏ Tap out the syllables and check each syllable for a vowel

❏ Try to visualize what the word looks like

❏ Use another piece of paper or the margin to spell the word several ways

❏ Use words I know to spell other words

❏ Use a portable word wall

❏ Use the class word wall

❏ Refer to the tricky words and homophone lists

❏ Use a dictionary

❏ Use a thesaurus

❏ If I know I can find the word quickly, I might _____

❏ If I think it will take me some time to find the correct spelling, I wait until editing then I

❏ During proofreading and editing, I ask a friend to edit with me

❏ During proofreading and editing, I add words to my portable word wall that I think I will use again.

If I were to give advice to a younger student about spelling, I would tell that writer:

_____

_____

Spelling Consciousness

Model the Focus Point

When I write my first drafts, I know spelling is very important, but I don't want to stop and look up how to spell a word—that would interrupt my train of thought. So when I am unsure of my spelling, I draw a line under the word or put a small *sp* to remind myself to check the spelling later when I am editing. In my title, *Odyssey on the Tracks*, I'm not exactly sure how to spell *odyssey,* so I will underline it to remind myself to check the spelling when I finish writing. *Odyssey* is a great word that makes this sound more like an adventure. I wouldn't want to miss out on a great word like that just because I am not sure how to spell it. I am also wondering about *fascinating* in the first sentence. I am drawing a line under that word as well. Spelling consciousness means you pay attention to spelling and give yourself reminders to check words, but you keep on reaching for the richest, most interesting words possible.

> **Modeled Writing Sample**
>
> <u>Odyssey</u> on the Tracks
>
> A 29-hour train trip was not only fun but also <u>fascinating</u>. When my boys and I <u>ascended</u> into the coach, I could see their <u>hesitation</u>. Maybe it would have been more convenient to fly to Glacier National Park, but the scenery we could glimpse out the window of the train made this our best vacation ever.

 TURN AND TALK Partners, think together—why does it make sense to continue writing on the first draft instead of stopping to look up unknown words in a dictionary? What did I do to note possible misspellings? Why is it wise to use this strategy during drafting?

SUM IT UP When writing a first draft, if you're uncertain about the spelling of a word, quickly underline it or write *sp* above the word. You can look up the spellings of tricky words after you write.

Guided Practice

Place student writing on the overhead projector. You can use the sample on page 188 or select a writing sample from your class. Choose a sample that would benefit from a careful check of spelling. If the author is a student, invite him or her to read aloud.

 TURN AND TALK Briefly discuss the meaning of the piece, and think of a compliment to offer the writer. Did the author pay attention to spelling? How could you tell? Which words should have been underlined or marked with *sp*?

> *Head Lice*
>
> I have this teacher She is really nice. But some time I think She has head lice. She itches all day. And the last time for head lice check She got sent home from school. I want tell you more but it is not cool. The day She come back She had no hair and her head was bear. I think to my self how did She get the lice. I kept on thinking untell I new that I was not nice because I'm the one who gave her the lice.
>
> By: Samantha

SUM IT UP To a class editing chart, add "Underline or write *sp* near any words with spellings you're unsure of."

Write *sp* above words with spellings you don't know. Keep writing and check the tricky spellings after you've finished.

DAY 3 Independent Practice

Select a rough draft from a writing folder and then model rereading to look for evidence of spelling consciousness, marking *sp* or underlining. Then have students practice by looking through their writing folders for evidence of spelling consciousness.

 PEER EDIT How would you define "spelling consciousness?" Why is it important, and how can it help your writing? Remember to mark words as you write so you don't break your train of thought. You can go back and check tricky spellings after your ideas are on paper.

 SUM IT UP During writing, quickly underline or write *sp* above uncertain spellings. After writing, return to verify or correct spelling.

✔ Assess the Learning

- As writers begin working, go around and note on a class record-keeping grid the students whose papers include underlining, or *sp*, or other evidence of spelling consciousness.

- Meet with students individually, asking them to talk about spelling consciousness and tell how it helps their writing. Provide extra support for those who still aren't clear about checking for spelling as they write.

🔗 Link the Learning

- Students might record correct spellings of tricky words in alphabetized multipage personal dictionaries. The problem area of a word should be highlighted, underlined, bolded, or broken into helpful chunks to aid spelling (e.g., *neighbor: neigh bor*).

- Celebrate texts that use rich, robust vocabulary rather than words that might be "easy." Encourage students to choose the best word for the sentence, not the word that is easiest to spell. Great books can help students see the power of word choice, such as *Shrek*, or *Amos and Boris* by William Steig, *Tuck Everlasting* by Natalie Babbit, *A Drop of Water* by Walter Wick, *Under the Quilt of Night* by Deborah Hopkinson, or *Owl Moon* by Jane Yolen.

- Provide multiple resources for checking spelling. You might also remind students of the pitfalls of spell-checking programs on the computer. They often miss words that may be spelled correctly in a different sentence but are misused and therefore misspelled in the particular sentence. We know these potentially tricky words as homophones.

Portable Word Walls

DAY 1   Model the Focus Point

Note: Prepare this writing sample in advance. As the lesson begins, pass out copies of the tool, Portable Word Wall, page 151.

> This resource is called a portable word wall. We are going to place it in a sheet protector because you will find it is one of your favorite writing tools. What's so great about this is that you keep it in your writing folder and can quickly check the spellings of these words without taking up writing time. It is so quick to use, and you won't lose your train of thought while you write. Let's use our portable word walls and quickly check this piece of writing. I notice *before* may be a challenge. Check the *b* section of portable word wall. If it isn't there, this writer should underline and then continue writing. In sentence two, I am concerned about *very*. That is a high-frequency word. I will use my portable word wall for that word as well.

Modeled Writing Sample

Befor tonight, I had always made shure I had enuff time to finish my homework. But I was vary nervous about writing this essay, and I had put it off untill the last minute. I knew that I wuld never do this again!

 TURN AND TALK Portable word walls contain high-frequency words that are commonly misspelled. How are you going to use it during drafting and again during editing?

 SUM IT UP Use a personal word wall to quickly check words during writing. After writing, use the personal word wall to proofread and edit spelling.

DAY 2   Guided Practice

Place student writing on the overhead projector. Use the writing sample on page 187 or one from your class. If the author is one of your students, invite him or her to read the selection to the class. Hand out the portable word wall, page 151, to your student editors.

By Darby

Penguin Bodys

Penguins are not your ordinarey birds. There feathers may look like fur, but thy are, in fact, feathers. There mostly black on top and white on there bellies. From the sky, the black looks like the bottom of the water and from below, there white bellies look like ice or just blend with the sky.

Most other birds use there feathers to fly. Not the penguins. Thay can't fly but are good simmers. There long, outer feathers help keep the water out. Under the outer feathers is a layer of down. Anuther layer comes below the down. However, its not feathers, but blubber. The blubber helps them stay warm in the cold waters of Antarctica. Most birds wouldn't want to live there.

Short legs are set back on there bodys. This makes them sway back and forth when they walk. Some call this waddling. Thay look awkward on land. This is one reason why thay slide on there bellys. Once thay dive into the sea, there good divers, thay become gracefull.

 TURN AND TALK Offer a compliment to this writer. What can you say about the meaning of the text? Proofread and edit for spelling using the portable word wall. What strategies can you use to spell words that do not appear on the wall?

 SUM IT UP To a class editing chart, add "Use portable word walls both during and after writing."

Writers use portable word walls to check spelling quickly during writing and more carefully after writing.

DAY 3 Independent Practice

Select a piece of writing that includes words frequently misspelled by fourth and fifth graders. Demonstrate using the portable word wall to proofread and edit. Then give writers time to select a piece to proofread and edit, consulting their portable word walls.

 PEER EDIT Point out places in your writing where you used your portable word wall to correct misspelled words. Then, recheck your partner's work using the word wall as a resource.

 SUM IT UP A portable word wall can help you spell high-frequency words. You can use it quickly while you write, and you can check it very carefully when your draft is complete.

✔ Assess the Learning

- Students can self-assess by putting small sticky notes near words that give them more trouble than others. Celebrate when students remove the sticky notes to show mastery in spelling these words.

- Use a class record-keeping grid to document students' use of portable word walls both during and after drafting writing and meet with them to discern how effectively they are using these tools. Continue to model using these tools for students who need extra support.

Link the Learning

- Students can create context sentences for troublesome high-frequency words, particularly homophones, such as *there, their, they're.* Context sentences can be kept in a section of their writer's notebooks. Students can use the Spelling Reference: Tricky Words and Homophones in addition to their portable word walls when creating their context sentences.

- Have students write letters to their parents explaining how they use the portable word walls to strengthen their writing. They can take their letters home, along with copies of their personal word walls, to support the writing process at home.

- Encourage the use of portable word walls during science and social studies to integrate spelling awareness of high-frequency words into all writing tasks.

- While focusing on a specific area of study, such as photosynthesis, create content word walls for both the class wall and for portable, personal use. Students are responsible for correct spelling of content words as long as the teaching focus remains the same. When the content focus shifts, for example, to the study of clouds, retire the previous content words and create a new content word wall and portable word wall for independent use.

Margin Spelling

DAY 1 Model the Focus Point

Today I am going to use a strategy called margin spelling to help me spell words correctly. I know in a final draft we don't write in the margins of the paper, but while I write a rough draft, I can use the margin to help me spell. When I come across a word with a spelling I don't know, I try out a few spellings in the margin. If I recognize that one of the spellings is correct, I'll cross out the incorrect one and put in the correct spelling. If I am still confused, I'll just cross them all out and put *sp* above the word in my writing. I can go back and check the spelling of that tricky word later.

TURN AND TALK Partners, how did using the margin help me spell tricky words? What other strategies did you see me use to spell words that I was unsure of?

SUM IT UP Use margin spelling during writing to quickly try different spellings of tricky words. Choose the spelling that looks correct, or mark the word to check later.

Modeled Writing Sample

My favorite time to work

is long before anyone else

is awake. The silence^{sp}   silense

in the house helps me

^{sp}
consentrate. All I can hear are   concentrate

faint "morning house" silence

sounds: the sighs of my boys

in their sleep, the ticking of

an old clock, consentrate^{sp}   skitering

and the skittering^{sp} of my cats'   skittering

claws on the hardwood floor.

DAY 2 Guided Practice

Place student writing on the overhead projector. Use the sample from the Appendix, page 177, or a writing sample from your class. Student authors may wish to read aloud to the class.

TURN AND TALK Talk about the meaning of the writing with your partner and share a compliment. Can you see the writer "trying out" different spellings of words in the margin? If you were this writer's spelling buddy, what specific feedback would you offer to strengthen the spelling? The overall paper?

SUM IT UP To a class editing chart, add "Use margin spelling."

Margin spelling is a quick way to help spell words as you write. Try to spell a tricky word a few different ways in the margin.

Model how to scan a paper for potential spelling errors. Try a few margin spellings for a tricky word on a large sheet of paper so students can see your various attempts. Then, turn the responsibility over to student editors to review their own writing folders.

 PEER EDIT Compare margin spellings with your partner. Does margin spelling help you with spellings of tricky words? In what ways? Together, try a few more margin spellings for words that you may have misspelled.

 SUM IT UP Writers use margin spelling to help themselves identify correct spelling or remind themselves to check a word later.

✔ Assess the Learning

- Student editors write their names on a sticky-note and record one example of margin spelling attempts. Collect notes on chart paper. Analyze the error patterns that you observe. Focus on these spelling patterns in your spelling instruction.

- Note which writers are using margin spelling and thinking in terms of common spelling patterns. Coach students who need extra support. Make sure to emphasize the importance of making serious attempts at spelling rather than just writing down groups of letters in the margin.

∞ Link the Learning

- Challenge students to choose words that truly make their writing sparkle rather than the words that are simply "easy." Celebrate strategies that students use to spell these powerful words. Read from mentor texts—or have students choose passages to share—with vocabulary that inspires students to choose precise words, even if they are difficult to spell.

- Have fun with margin spellings by sharing tricky words and having partners try to come up with at least three potentially correct spellings.

- Model using margin spelling while creating charts in science and social studies.

- Help students remember to celebrate their margin spellings when they edit by keeping track of the number of correct letters they had in a word.

Homophones

 DAY 1 | **Model the Focus Point**

Note: Pass out copies of the Tricky Words Homophones reference in the Tools section, page 152.

As writers, we always focus on meaning. In doing so, we need to be especially careful with homophones, those pesky words that sound alike but have different spellings and meanings, or our readers will get confused. We are going to practice using a Tricky Words tool that you will want to keep handy in your writing folder or in your writer's notebook. I wrote, *weighting an our...* **I want to check** *weighting* **and** *our.* **Those are homophones. On the Tricky Words page, I will check the context sentences to be sure I selected the correct homophone. Oops! I needed to write** *waiting,* **because this isn't about how much I weigh. I need to write** *hour* **because this is about the time. I also want to check** *four.* **That is a homophone as well. Partners, use your tool and help me check the rest of this writing.**

> **Modeled Writing Sample**
>
> I have been weighting an our four the plumbers to arrive. My faucet is leeking and I don't no what to do. They're schedule must be really busy but I am busy two. This isn't fare.

TURN AND TALK Writers, think together. Homophones are not picked up by the computer spell-check. How can you be sure to use the correct homophone during writing? How might you use this tool?

SUM IT UP Homophones are words that sound the same but are spelled differently and have different meanings. Writers need to pay attention and use these correctly or readers will get confused.

DAY 2 | **Guided Practice**

Place student writing on the overhead projector. Use the sample in the Appendix, page 187, or one from your class. Student authors may wish to read aloud to the class.

> By Darby
>
> Penguin Bodys
>
> Penguins are not your ordinarey birds. There feathers may look like fur, but thy are, in fact, feathers. There mostly black on top and white on there bellies. From the sky, the black looks like the bottom of the water and from below, there white bellies look like ice or just blend with the sky.
>
> Most other birds use there feathers to fly. Not the pengiuns. Thay can't fly but are good simmers. There long, outer feathers help keep the water out. Under the outer feathers is a layer of down. Anuther layer comes below the down. However, its not feathers, but blubber. The blubber helps them stay warm in the cold waters of Antarctica. Most birds wuoldn't want to live there.
>
> Short legs are set back on there bodys. This makes them sway back and forth when they walk. Some call this waddling. Thay look awkward on land. This is one reason why thay slide on there bellys. Once thay dive into the sea, there good divers, thay become gracefull.

TURN AND TALK Talk about the meaning of the writing, and come up with a compliment for the author. If you were this writer's editing partner, what would you do to help with homophones? Use your Tricky Words tool and decide what this writer needs to do.

 SUM IT UP To a class editing chart, add "Watch for Homophones."

It is really important to pay attention to homophones and select the correct word to match your meaning. Use your Tricky Words tool.

Model how to scan a paper for homophones, placing a sticky note on pages where you find them. Show how you check the homophone by using the Tricky Word tool. Have student editors review their own writing folders for correct use of homophones.

PEER EDIT Share the homophones you identified in your writing and the context sentences that helped you identify the correct form.

SUM IT UP Homophones are important words that writers need to notice. These words sound the same but they are spelled differently and have different meanings.

✔ Assess the Learning

- Gather writing folders or writer's notebooks and assess your students' understanding of homophones.

- Have students create their own sentences for homophones in their writer's notebooks. Collect the notebooks and assess the sentences for clarity of understanding.

Link the Learning

- Have teams create posters featuring commonly used homophones, e.g., *there, their, they're; your, you're; which, witch; to, too, two; weather, whether; past, passed; pair, pare, pear; its, it's,* and so on. Have students include context sentences or drawings to help writers remember which meanings go with which spellings. Post the posters on the walls for reference.

- Provide cloze activities with homophones omitted. Have partners think together and use their Tricky Words pages to select the correct homophones.

- Have students dramatize homophones and their meanings or make up hand signals to go with each homophone.

- Examine mentor books for homophones in context. A few examples: *Miss Alaineus: A Vocabulary Disaster* by Debra Frasier, *The True Story of the Three Little Pigs* by John Scieszka, *The King Who Rained* by Fred Gwynne; *A Chocolate Moose for Dinner, A Series of Unfortunate Events* by Lemony Snicket.

Pulling It All Together

For learning to be long lasting, learners need opportunities to explore their understandings in more than one context. The Power Burst Lessons and Pulling It All Together Cycles are designed to provide interactive experiences in which students can review conventions and mechanics they have recently explored in a cycle. These experiences are not designed to teach new content but rather to review and support the transfer of learning to other contexts.

There are two parts to this section:

Power Burst Lessons: These are learning experiences that fit nicely into small windows of time. When you have 10 minutes, slip in one of these interactive experiences to review recently addressed conventions and mechanics.

Pulling It All Together Cycles: These are fully developed cycles that are linked to the Yearlong Planner (see the interior cover of this book) and designed to tie together multiple points of learning. These cycles provide intensive review of three weeks of learning within the context of an authentic writing experience intended for a real audience.

Power Burst Lesson: Secret Sentences

To create "secret sentences," write each word and punctuation mark of a familiar sentence on individual sheets of paper, one word or punctuation mark per piece. Have teams of students (each student holds one piece of paper) move themselves around to arrange their words and punctuation into a sentence, checking for a beginning capital letter, punctuation marks, and that the sentence makes sense. Groups discuss the strategies they used to create sentences and how recent cycles for patterns of grammar use or punctuation helped them unlock the secret sentence.

You might begin with sentences culled from familiar texts, including content-area texts and selections used for read-alouds. As students gain experience with secret sentences, branch out to less familiar sentences that provide a review of grammatical structures, recently learned mechanics, spelling rules and conventions, or complex sentences linked with connecting words and commas.

"Secret sentences" challenge students' understanding of grammar, punctuation, capitalization, and word order. These fourth graders solve the sentence, "Good writers reread for each editing point." As their skills sharpen, students can solve increasingly complex sentences, such as the following:

- **Good writers focus on audience and reread for each editing point.**
- **Good writers, focused on audience, reread carefully for each editing point.**
- **With their readers in mind, good writers reread carefully for each editing point.**

Power Burst Lesson: Scavenger Hunt

Use a piece of text reproduced on a transparency to demonstrate how to survey a selection for periods, question marks, commas, pronouns, subjects and verbs, and so on. Select a convention or aspect of mechanics that you have studied in a recent cycle and count to see how many times it occurs in the text.

Once students are familiar with the scavenger hunt idea, have individuals, partners, or reading teams survey whole-class reading selections, small-group guided reading selections, weekly magazines, newspapers, and so on, keeping a tally of their findings and collecting terrific sentences to display in the room.

Students will enjoy scavenging for commas in William Steig's *Shrek* or Walter Wick's *A Drop of Water*. As students continue to gain more skill in conducting scavenger hunts for differing purposes, encourage students to work with partners to conduct a scavenger hunt through their own writing folders.

Power Burst Lesson: Combining Sentences

Research suggests that students become more proficient writers when they learn to combine short sentences into longer, more complex structures. At times, students often produce sentences sounding something like:

Lions are strong. They have big paws. They are the kings of the jungle.

In "Combining Sentences" the objective is for students to get involved in the action. Place short sentences written on sentence strips in a pocket chart, and then show how you can cut up the sentences and create richer, more interesting statements. Be sure to place punctuation marks and connecting words (*and, but, although*) on individual sentence strips so their presence is very obvious. Your creations might sound something like this:

The <u>big paws</u> and strong body of the waiting lion made it clear that he was <u>king of the jungle</u>.

With his <u>big paws</u> in a relaxed pose, the <u>strong</u> body of the lion made it clear that he was <u>king of the jungle</u>.

Lions have <u>big paws</u> and <u>strong</u> bodies that earned them a reputation as <u>king of the jungle</u>.

Lions have <u>big paws,</u> but it is their <u>strong</u> body that earned them the title <u>king of the jungle</u>.

Guided Practice

Provide partners with two short sentences on sentence strips. Encourage them to cut the sentences apart with the goal of combining the sentences, adding more words and creating one sentence that is longer and more interesting. Point out that adding commas and connecting words will help them as they combine sentences. Have them post their new sentences in a pocket chart.

Alternates

- Provide students with compound sentences written on sentence strips. Have them cut the sentences apart and create two shorter sentences.

- Have students search through favorite books to find compound sentences (a sentence with two independent clauses linked by a connecting word). Then, they write their sentences out on a sentence strip and then rewrite them as two shorter sentences.

Power Burst Lesson: Pin It Up!

Designate bulletin board space with engaging headings that invite students to add examples from literature they have read. Create space for titles such as "Powerful Verbs," "Precise Nouns," "Fabulous Prepositional Phrases," "Great Sentence Openers," "Realistic Dialogue," and so on. You might start with one heading and add others as more lesson cycles are introduced.

Model for students how to find and add examples to the bulletin board. While reading aloud, for example, stop at a sentence with a powerful verb and say something like,

> "When I read this sentence, this verb helped me get such a clear picture of what was happening in the story. The author chose a precise and powerful verb! I want to remember it, because sometimes when I read great books, I find ideas for my own writing. I will place a sticky note at this point in the book so I remember to come back and put this sentence up for display."

Then copy the sentence onto a sentence strip and add it to the bulletin board.

During independent reading time, encourage students to be on the lookout for examples of powerful verbs, precise nouns, or your current bulletin board topics. They can mark those examples in their books with sticky notes, share with partners after reading, and then add their most powerful examples to the board.

Power Burst Lesson: Stretch and Shorten

As a lead-in to this activity, read aloud from and celebrate a text such as Gary Paulsen's *Dogsong*, in which the author expertly crafts short sentences for maximum impact and emotion.

Write each word of a two-word sentence on a separate index card and provide students with these cards.

Examples:

Geese waddle.

Horses thunder.

Babies toddle.

Students can work in pairs or small groups to stretch the sentences by adding words or phrases. You might focus the stretching by asking students to add certain elements, such as an adjective, an opener with a comma, an interrupter, a closer, an adverb, a prepositional phrase, dialogue, and so on. As students write their sentences, remind them to use correct punctuation. The key is to start with a powerful core and then build the sentence from there.

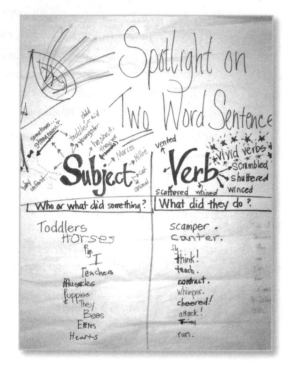

Students can also shorten sentences. Provide groups with a piece of text with three or four long sentences. Ask them to think about the impact of shortening one of the sentences to just two words. How can sentence shortening make their writing more powerful? After groups have each shortened one sentence, have them share their results and discuss how shortening particular sentences affected their writing.

Extension Idea: Headlines

Newspaper headlines are often incomplete sentences, meant to quickly convey a message. Let students know that, in this exercise, their job is to turn headlines into interesting sentences that convey clear messages.

Display a few headlines from a newspaper or magazine and ask students to write sentences of their own based on the headlines. Students can share their sentences with classmates after they focus on both the message and the mechanics.

Use this opportunity to discuss the parts of a complete sentence.

Extension

Have students write headlines for classroom studies and school events, then create a feature article to go with the headline. Publish their articles as a classroom newsletter for parents.

Power Burst Lesson: Check It!

The best editing checklists are the ones you make yourself. Editing checklists help writers hone in on the writing traits they feel are most important and give writers a sense of purpose as they edit their writing with an audience in mind.

Begin by identifying an authentic writing purpose, such as an invitation to a school event, a letter to parents, a book review, and so on. Students can choose this type of authentic writing from their writing folders.

Elicit students' ideas for an editing checklist suited for the audience and purpose for their piece of writing. Post the checklist and have students test it with their writing. Provide copies for individuals to use as they prepare their work for an audience. Ask students how editing checklists geared toward particular writing pieces may vary; for example, how is a checklist for a persuasive letter going to vary from writing an informational report?

Power Burst Lesson: Punctuation Power

Write sentences *without* punctuation and place them in a pocket chart. We suggest using sentences that challenge students to apply concepts from recent cycles, such as the following:

Apostrophes
- Include sentences with plural and singular possessives that need apostrophes, such as, *Barneys doghouse is tucked under the cover by the patio* and *The dogs leashes are hanging on the hook by the door.*
- Add sentences with irregular plurals, such as, *The childrens books were in their backpacks.*
- Incorporate sentences with possessive pronouns and contractions, such as *I dont like its flavor.*

Commas
- Add sentences that require commas in a series, such as, *He was tall dignified and walked with a limp* and *The avenue was lined with blossoming trees gardens filled with flowers and white fences.*
- Post a sentence with an interrupter and have the students insert commas.
- Include sentences with dialogue: *Stop bellowed the mom a car is coming.*
- Incorporate compound and complex sentences, such as, *Stop or I'll scream* or *The lion who thought he was the king lived on the open plain but the meerkat had an intricate series of tunnels for its home.*
- Include sentences with introductory phrases, such as, *Of course it had to rain on our field day.*

Grammar
- Place sentences in the chart with omissions for pronouns, verbs, and so on.

Spelling
- Place sentences in the chart with misspelled words and have students work in pairs to edit the spelling.

Pulling It All Together Cycle #1: Request Letter

End Punctuation of Four Kinds of Sentences • Spelling Consciousness • Proofreading and Editing During and After Writing

DAY 1 Model Writing for an Audience

I am writing a request letter to our gym teacher to ask for space in the gym for our science fair. We've been working hard on end punctuation, proofreading during and after our writing, and thinking about our spelling. It's makes sense to consider these things, because it's an important letter. I start my letter with *Dear*. Here's my first sentence: *Our class is holding a science fair!* The science fair is exciting, but I don't think I need to use an exclamation point. Let's change it to a period. Now I'm making my request. It's a question, so I need a question mark. *Could we please borrow the gym on Wensday?* Hmmm, that day of the week is the hardest one for me to spell. I don't want to stop writing to check the spelling, so I'll put a little *sp* above the word to remember to check it after I write.

Modeled Writing Sample

Dear Ms. Ruddy,

Our class is holding a science fair. Our room is too small for all our projects. They are amazing! Could we please borrow the gym on Wednesday? We'll clean up after school on Thursday.

Sincerely,

Ms. Brent's class

TURN AND TALK Writers, let's talk about my writing. How did I know which end punctuation to use? What strategy did I use when I wasn't sure how to spell a word? Tell your partner about one strategy you use to check spelling.

CREATE AUTHENTIC PURPOSE Have students write request letters. They might ask to borrow something from a friend, put a hold on a book in the library, ask a parent to provide a treat for a special day at school, and so on. Remind students to proofread and edit both during and after writing and to check end punctuation and spelling.

ASSESS THE LEARNING As students work, monitor which students need assistance with choosing the correct end punctuation, paying attention to word spellings, and proofreading during and after writing. Provide additional support for those who need it.

SUM IT UP Writers, we wrote polite requests to ask for things, and the careful attention that we paid to our writing shows the sincerity of our request. When you check your spelling as you write, proofread both during and after you write, and use the correct punctuation, your writing is polished and professional.

DAY 2 Guided Practice

MODEL: APPLY THE LEARNING TO DAILY WRITING Select a piece of modeled writing and approach it with a fresh editing eye as you check on end punctuation. Think aloud about using exclamation points to emphasize emotion or excitement, correctly framing questions, and so on. Explicitly model proofreading and editing both during and after drafting.

 TURN AND TALK Writers, why did I focus on editing both during and after writing? What strategies did I use to select the correct end punctuation? How can you use those strategies in your own writing?

 CREATE AUTHENTIC PURPOSES Have students select pieces from their writing folders to reread with a focus on punctuation and spelling. Encourage them to mark words they are unsure of to check later. If their end punctuation is correct, students can try turning a statement into a question for emphasis.

 ASSESS THE LEARNING Use your class record-keeping grid to track students who may need additional support in utilizing spelling consciousness and correctly employing end punctuation. Meet individually or in groups with those who need extra help.

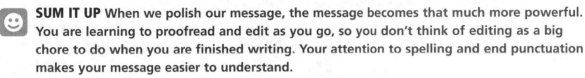 **SUM IT UP** When we polish our message, the message becomes that much more powerful. You are learning to proofread and edit as you go, so you don't think of editing as a big chore to do when you are finished writing. Your attention to spelling and end punctuation makes your message easier to understand.

DAY 3 Support and Extend the Learning

Select experiences that will best support your learners:

- Create a bulletin board with the headings *interrogative, declarative, exclamatory,* and *imperative.* Have students add sentences to the bulletin board in the correct categories. Sentences can come from students' own writing and/or from literature and content-area books. Remind them to select strong examples that show the power of using each type of sentence.

- Have students contribute to a bulletin board of "spelling puzzlers"—tricky words about which they were unsure but used their spelling consciousness and reference sources to spell correctly. Have them add the correct spellings to the display.

- Students can complete on-the-go editing by having checklists close at hand. Have them create bookmarks or similar "small checklists" that they can easily use at a glance to strengthen their writing.

- Students may enjoy playing "stump the editor." Have pairs write a sentence that includes an error from this cycle of lessons. They can trade sentences with another pair and edit. Did they identify the intentional error? Could they think of another way to strengthen the sentence?

Pulling It All Together Cycle #2: Summary

Complete Sentences vs. Fragments • Portable Word Walls • Checklist for Focused Proofreading and Editing

DAY 1   **Model Writing for an Audience**

I am writing a summary for our timeline of U. S. history. We've been working on writing complete sentences, using portable word walls and a checklist for proofreading and editing. I'll use all these strategies as I write. In my first sentence, I want to use the word *found*, but I'm not sure if the */ou/* is spelled with *ow* or *ou*. I'll check my portable word wall—there it is, *f-o-u-n-d*. Now here's my second sentence: *After 10 long weeks at sea.* Wait—a sentence needs a subject and a verb. This group of words doesn't have either; it's an introduction to a sentence. So I need to combine it with the next group of words. (Continue writing a sample as shown, modeling writing complete sentences and checking word spellings with your word wall.) **Now I am finished. I am going to focus my proofreading and editing by using a checklist instead of looking at all the errors at once. The first point on my checklist asks: Does every sentence have a correct end punctuation mark? So that's what I'll check on the first rereading.**

> **Modeled Writing Sample**
>
> 1492: Christopher Columbus Sees Land!
>
> On October 12, 1492, a sailor gazed toward the horizon from his ship and spotted land. After ten long weeks at sea, Columbus saw the New World. The following day, he and his crew planted the Spanish flag on this small island in the Bahamas. Did you know that Columbus explored other lands on his journeys?

TURN AND TALK Writers, what strategies did you see me use to write complete sentences? Why do you think I focused on one editing point at a time instead of looking for all of the errors? How did this help me keep my writing more organized?

CREATE AUTHENTIC PURPOSES Create opportunities for students to write summaries of content-area learning. Remind students to keep—and use—copies of their portable word walls to check to be sure their sentences are complete, and to use a focused editing checklist to guide their proofreading and editing.

ASSESS THE LEARNING As students work, use a class record-keeping grid to note those who may need extra assistance with utilizing the word wall, writing complete sentences, and editing in a focused way. For those needing support, provide individual conferences or small-group work.

SUM IT UP Writers, a summary is a focused piece of writing that relays important information. Using correct spelling, complete sentences and editing carefully ensures that we convey important information in a way that makes sense to our readers.

DAY 2 Guided Practice

MODEL: APPLY THE LEARNING TO DAILY WRITING Select a piece of modeled writing and reread it, checking the spelling with your portable word wall. Identify subjects and verbs in sentences to be sure they are complete. Finally, with a checklist, carefully reread for each editing point.

 TURN AND TALK Writers, talk about my editing strategies. Why do you think it was helpful to edit for one point at a time? What editing points do you think would be most important to include on a checklist? Why do you think so?

 CREATE AUTHENTIC PURPOSES Students go through their writing folders to select pieces for focused editing, paying careful attention to spelling and writing complete sentences. Encourage them to keep their portable word walls by their sides as they edit. Students could also edit with partners.

 ASSESS THE LEARNING As students reread and edit, use a class record-keeping grid to note those who need extra help with writing complete sentences, spelling words correctly, and editing with a focused checklist. Gather those who need assistance and provide support as they work through their writing.

 SUM IT UP A summary ties up important information, and if we want our readers to understand it, our writing must be clear. Now we are editors with a clear map to guide us—an editing checklist. The portable word wall is another tool that helps our writing shine. Carefully crafted sentences make our writing much easier to understand.

DAY 3 Support and Extend the Learning

Select experiences that will best support your learners:

- Not all fragments are "bad!" Help students find examples of sentence fragments in writing that add emphasis, make the writing sound more natural, and so on. Celebrate the use of purposeful fragments by reading these examples in class and posting them for inspiration.

- Portable word walls need to be portable—students should avoid overloading them. You might suggest that students make "category word walls," such as science words or words about the American Revolution.

- Students may enjoy teaching younger students how to use editing checklists. Have them create checklists that cover the basics of editing for younger students. Watch as your students teach their editing buddies how to read for each editing point, such as capital letters and end punctuation.

- Students create posters highlighting editing tips to share with younger students. Posters could show before-and-after sentences with simple editing rules that are easy to remember. Bold colors and illustrations make the work more memorable. Mnemonics could be included as well (_Big Elephants Can Always Use Scrambled Eggs_ to spell _BECAUSE_.).

Pulling It All Together Cycle #3: Recipe

Commas and Connecting Words in Compound Sentences • Adverbs and Adverb Phrases
• Copyediting Symbols to Edit Writing

DAY 1 | Model Writing for an Audience

Note: You may need to point out that the subjects of the sentences are the inferred "you."

I want to write a healthy recipe. We've been working on using commas to connect sentences and choosing adverbs to make our writing more precise. I'll consider these strategies as I write. Let's start with the first step. *Cut the pepper in half. Clean out the seeds and the gunk from inside.* I could use the word *and* to connect these short sentences. *The next step is to cut the carrot and celery into sticks.* I want to tell the cook how to use the knife, so I'll use the adverb *carefully*. That's an important word for using a knife! Now I'll edit. I forgot to capitalize the first word of the third step. I'll underline the letter three times and write *CAP* by it. I'll remember to fix that before I put the recipe in our class recipe book. Uh oh, I forgot a word in the last step. I wrote *Pull out the and dip them in dressing.* What do I want to pull out? The vegetables! I'll put this little mark—a caret—to show that I am missing a word. I can put that word in when I make my final copy.

> **Modeled Writing Sample**
>
> **Veggies in an Edible Bowl!**
>
> Ingredients: 1 pepper, washed; 1 carrot; 1 stalk of celery; salad dressing
>
> Directions:
>
> 1. Cut the pepper in half and clean out the seeds and gunk from the inside.
>
> 2. Carefully cut the carrot and celery into strips.
>
> 3. Pour salad dressing in the bottom of the pepper bowl. Put the vegetables inside.
>
> 4. Pull out the vegetables and dip them in the dressing. Then, you can eat the bowl!

TURN AND TALK Writers, talk about what you saw me doing to connect two short sentences. What did I need to do to put them together? What adverbs and adverb phrases made my writing easier to understand? With your partner, think of another place I could use an adverb.

CREATE AUTHENTIC PURPOSE Students can work with partners to create recipes of their own for a healthy recipe book. Remind them that recipes have ingredients lists and ordered steps. Encourage them to combine short sentences, use adverbs to make steps clearer, and use copyediting symbols as they edit their work.

ASSESS THE LEARNING While students work with partners, circulate with a class record-keeping grid to note those who need assistance combining sentences, using adverbs, and proofreading with copyediting symbols. Provide assistance in an individual or small-group setting.

SUM IT UP Copyediting symbols are like signs—signs that point the way to better writing! Combining small sentences helps make our writing flow. It sounds more natural, the way that people speak. Adverbs add even more detail to our writing. Our recipes will be easy to follow!

DAY 2 Guided Practice

MODEL: APPLY THE LEARNING TO DAILY WRITING Choose a previous modeled writing to proofread and edit. Use copyediting symbols showing how these are signals for improving the writing. Find short sentences to combine into sentences that flow, emphasizing that those sentences sound natural and add variety. Put sticky notes near verbs, and model choosing the verbs that could use adverbs for clarifying.

 TURN AND TALK Writers, how did using copyediting symbols make my job as an editor easier? What was the effect of combining short sentences into a longer one? Of adding adverbs?

 CREATE AUTHENTIC PURPOSES Ask students to select a piece of their writing to reread with an eye toward identifying short sentences that would sound more natural if combined. Have them mark verbs with sticky notes to choose ones that need "beefing up" by using adverbs. Provide a chart of copy editor's symbols to assist students.

 ASSESS THE LEARNING Keep a list of students who need additional assistance with combining sentences, using adverbs and adverb phrases, and using editing marks during proofreading. Careful scaffolding will assist these students to use the strategies.

 SUM IT UP Writers, you are using copyediting symbols to show where you need to return to make your writing even better. Combining sentences can make short, choppy sentences sound more natural; and adverbs can make powerful verbs even stronger. Your editing skills are getting sharper and sharper.

DAY 3 Support and Extend the Learning

Select experiences that will best support your learners:

- Expand the idea of recipe writing to other process writing such as how to tie a shoe, how to set up a science experiment, how to serve a volleyball, and so on. Talk about how adverbs make the steps more specific and easier to follow.

- Provide students the opportunity to connect small sentences. Write several short sentences on sentence strips or index cards and mix them up. Students can then work in small groups to create sentences—either "serious" or "silly"—by combining sentences with connecting words and commas.

- Provide simple sentences for students to expand with adverbs and adverb phrases. Encourage them to think of the sentences as intriguing story openers. How can editors keep their readers "on the edge of their seats?" By adding intriguing adverbs! You can complete this activity orally as well. Gather students in a circle. Have them expand on a simple sentence by adding phrases as the sentence makes its way around the circle.

- Students can work in small groups to make copyediting symbols posters. Have them create small posters that feature one symbol each. The poster can show a sentence both "before" and "after" to illustrate how helpful copyediting symbols can be to students' writing.

Pulling It All Together Cycle #4: Book Review

Commas to Set Off Opener • Punctuation in Direct Quotations (Dialogue) • Subject-Verb Agreement for Singular Nouns and Pronouns

DAY 1   Model Writing for an Audience

Today, I'm writing a review of a book to add to our class library. I always try to do my best writing, but I want to pay attention to what we've been learning: using commas in openers, punctuating dialogue, and making subjects and verbs agree. I will start with an opener, *Desperate to help....* Notice that I put a comma after the opener. I want to make sure my subject and verb agree. I want to say, *Little Willy devises a plan.* Is it *devise*? Or *devises*? Willy is one person—a singular subject. I need to be sure the verb matches. I want to show how exciting the book was, so I'm including a bit of dialogue, "Go, Searchlight, go!" Those are words that someone said, so I am putting them in quotation marks. I put a comma before those words to set them apart from the sentence.

TURN AND TALK Talk with your partner about my writing. Find a singular subject and its verb. How can you tell that they agree? Why are there commas after *Desperate to help his grandfather*, *While his grandfather lies in bed*, and *As a reader*? What is the impact of putting a quotation in the review?

> **Modeled Writing Sample**
>
> Review of *Stone Fox*
>
> Desperate to help his grandfather, Little Willy devises an ingenious plan to win the $500 his grandfather needs for back taxes. While his grandfather lies in bed, Willy and his dog, Searchlight, enter a dog race with a prize of $500. As a reader, you can't help but cheer, "Go, Searchlight, go!" as they race for the finish line. This is an amazing story of loyalty and love.

CREATE AUTHENTIC PURPOSES Students can write book reviews. Encourage them to locate subjects and verbs and make sure they agree. Have them write a sentence with an opener that tells when, reminding them to include a comma. Finally, suggest that students include a piece of dialogue, either from themselves or from the books they review.

ASSESS THE LEARNING As students write, check to be sure that they are putting commas after openings, correctly punctuating dialogue, and making verbs agree with subjects. Note those who might need assistance in individual conferences or small groups.

SUM IT UP Writers, reviews are great tools for learning about books that we might want to read. And when reviews are well written, they are even easier to use. You made your reviews shine by correctly using commas in openers, punctuating dialogue, and having verbs agree with subjects in your sentences.

MODEL: APPLY THE LEARNING TO DAILY WRITING Model how to select a piece of writing from your writing folder and reread to check for commas after openings, punctuation with quotations, and subject-verb agreement with singular nouns and pronouns. As you identify these elements in the writing, think aloud and share your ideas about adjustments that you need to make.

 TURN AND TALK Writers, what did you see me do as I checked my writing? Talk about the way I checked subject-verb agreement. How can you tell when subjects and verbs don't agree?

 CREATE AUTHENTIC PURPOSES Have students look through their writing folders to find writing that might need a second look. Have partners work together to find openers in need of commas and to check subjects and verbs for agreement. If their work includes dialogue, they should check the punctuation. If not, encourage them to add dialogue that would make the writing vibrant.

 ASSESS THE LEARNING As partners work together, use the class record-keeping grid to identify students who may need extra support punctuating openers and dialogue and making subjects and verbs agree. These students might benefit from reteaching the strategies in this cycle.

 SUM IT UP Our list of strategies for focused proofreading and editing is growing. Now we know how to use commas after openings, make sure our subjects and verbs agree, and punctuate dialogue, or the exact words of speakers. Each strategy we learn improves our writing—and our readers' experiences!

DAY 3 **Support and Extend the Learning**

Select experiences that will best support your learners:

• Provide openers on index cards, such as *on a bright and cloudless morning, at the brink of a cliff, near the end of the long tunnel,* and so on. Students can use the openers for oral or written stories. Encourage students to write openers of their own for other students to use. Notice each of these openers begins with a preposition. Use Create Your Own Resource: Understanding Adverbs and Prepositional Phrases to develop openers.

• Celebrate the use of direct quotations by finding and sharing texts with dialogue that makes stories come to life. Read dialogue aloud with students to show them the impact dialogue can have on a story.

• Write dialogue from selections students are reading in class. Write the dialogue on sentence strips, omitting the punctuation. Challenge pairs to add the correct punctuation to the sentences.

• Provide sentences with plural nouns and pronouns as subjects. The challenge for students is to rewrite the sentences, changing plural nouns and pronouns to their singular versions and adjusting the verbs as necessary.

Pulling It All Together Cycle #5: Science Learning Log

Pronouns and Their Antecedents • Capitalize Proper Nouns vs. Lowercase Common Nouns • Apostrophe: Singular Possessive Nouns

DAY 1 **Model Writing for an Audience**

A learning log is a great way to keep track of ideas. I am going to write a learning log entry about a science experiment. We've been learning about pronouns, proper nouns, and possessive nouns, so I am going to pay special attention to these ideas in my writing. The first sentence tells what I was testing: *Newton's law of motion*. But Newton is a person's name, so I should capitalize his name and his law. Here's the first step of my experiment: *I blew it up and clamped it shut with a clothespin*. I'm missing something, though. Someone reading this won't know what I'm talking about! I need to replace the first pronoun with a noun. I double check the pronoun. Do I know what *it* refers to? Sure, it refers to the balloon. *I taped the balloon's long side to the straw*—let me write that down. I have to remember to use an apostrophe, because the *long side* belongs to the balloon. The *'s* comes after the word *balloon*.

> **Modeled Writing Sample**
>
> I Tested Newton's Third Law of Motion.
>
> 1. I blew up a balloon and clamped it shut with a clothespin.
>
> 2. I threaded string through a straw and taped the balloon's long side to the straw.
>
> 3. Two people held the string's ends, and I released the clothespin.
>
> 4. The balloon raced down the string.
>
> 5. When I released the pin, the air flew out, pushing the balloon in the opposite direction.

TURN AND TALK Talk about the writing with your partner. Look for pronouns and identify the nouns to which those pronouns refer. Find three possessive nouns—how can you tell they are possessives?

 CREATE AUTHENTIC PURPOSE Students can create entries in their learning logs in any subject area. Encourage them to include a pronoun in their writing and to be sure that that pronoun clearly refers to a particular noun. Remind them that singular possessives nouns—words that show ownership—need an apostrophe and *s*.

ASSESS THE LEARNING Use a class record-keeping grid to make note of students who may need assistance with possessives, pronouns and antecedents, and capitalization of proper nouns. Work with these students individually or in small groups.

SUM IT UP Learning logs are great tools to help us remember what we learned, but only if they make sense when we go back and read them later! So it's important that our writing is clear. When we use pronouns and possessives correctly, our writing makes sense. We need to capitalize proper nouns in our writing, too.

DAY 2 — Guided Practice

MODEL: APPLY THE LEARNING TO DAILY WRITING Choose a learning log or piece of writing from a previous modeled writing lesson. Mark pronouns with sticky notes and carefully read to check that each pronoun refers clearly to a noun. Be sure that singular nouns that show possession have an apostrophe and -*s*. Finally, look for proper nouns to be sure they are capitalized.

 TURN AND TALK Writers, how did I check to be sure each pronoun clearly refers to a noun? How did I repair any that were unclear?

 CREATE AUTHENTIC PURPOSES Have students peruse their writing folders to find content-area pieces for rereading. They can mark their pronouns with sticky notes and then check for clear referents. Add possessive and proper nouns to a focused editing checklist for students to use.

 ASSESS THE LEARNING As partners work together to reread their writing, identify any students who may need assistance with possessive nouns, pronouns and references, and proper nouns. Meet with these students individually or in groups to provide extra support.

SUM IT UP Writers, we are not only helping ourselves remember ideas, we are writing them well. We've learned how to use possessives and proper nouns. When we see a pronoun, we ask ourselves, "What noun is this pronoun referring to?" We know we should fix the sentence if we can't answer the question.

DAY 3 — Support and Extend the Learning

Select experiences that will best support your learners:

- Provide pairs of students with an index card on which you have written a common noun, such as *man, building, team, street, car,* and so on. Students should write as many proper nouns as they can that correspond to the common noun. Give a time limit to turn the activity into a contest! Allow time for students to share their responses.

- Students can use singular possessive nouns to create an illustrated food chain or food web. Students might, for example, draw a chain that includes a leaf, a worm, and a robin. Captions could read: *A leaf is a worm's meal. A robin's breakfast is a worm.*

- Students will enjoy creating riddles with pronouns in the answers—the antecedents will be in the questions. Examples:

    How do rabbits travel? They travel by hareplane.

    What clothing does a house wear? It wears an address.

    What did the sock say to the foot? You are putting me on!

    What does the invisible man drink? He drinks evaporated milk.

    What did mom wear when the basement flooded? She wore pumps!

Pulling It All Together Cycle #6: Poem

Verb Forms: Regular and Irregular • Verb Types: Action and Linking • Adjectives: Comparative and Superlative Forms

---

DAY 1 | **Model Writing for an Audience**

I am going to write a poem for our state display. During our writing and editing, we've spent a lot of time working on forms of verbs and on adjectives used to compare. I'll focus on those in my writing. In the first line, I'm using a linking verb—*am*. Is it the correct verb to use? I wouldn't say *I is Illinois* or *I are Illinois.* I've used the correct verb. Let's go on. *I am in the Midwest*. I'm thinking about using this linking verb, and I already used one in the same line. Now it's time for an action verb. *Dwell* is a lot more active than *am*. It makes it seem like the state is alive, because it has a home. In the second line, I'm writing about cities and how they grew. I used the word *rised*. But *rise* isn't a regular verb—I don't add *-ed* to make the past tense. Instead, I change *rise* to *rose*. In this line, I'm comparing the size of the Sears Tower to other buildings. I'm comparing more than two items, so I add the ending *-est* to tall.

> **Modeled Writing Sample**
>
> I am Illinois. I dwell in the Midwest.
>
> I am called the Prairie State, and cities rose from my rich soil.
>
> The Sears Tower springs up over all. It's the tallest building in North America.
>
> Violets grow in my fields, trout jump in my lakes, and eagles soar over my rivers.
>
> I am Illinois.

TURN AND TALK Writers, talk about my writing. Find a linking verb. Find an action verb. How are the verbs different? Imagine I had written about violets in the past tense. How would I have changed the verb *grow*? What about *jump*?

CREATE AUTHENTIC PURPOSES Ask students to work with partners to write poems about states. Remind students to vary the types of verbs they used and to be mindful of irregular verbs. Encourage them to think of something they can compare using the correct form of the adjective. (*The Sears Tower is the tallest building in North America.*)

ASSESS THE LEARNING Use your class record-keeping grid to note how best to support those who need assistance with their varying verb types and utilizing the correct forms of comparative adjectives.

SUM IT UP Writing would be dull if we used just one kind of verb, so we sprinkle different kinds into our writing—regular and irregular, linking and action. They aren't all easy to use, but you are close to mastering them! Using adjectives to compare gives your readers clear pictures of topics. Your poems create vivid word pictures, and that's the goal of poetry!

DAY 2 — Guided Practice

MODEL: APPLY THE LEARNING TO DAILY WRITING Choose a piece of modeled writing from a previous lesson. Mark each verb with a sticky note. Pause to ask questions such as "Would an action verb work better here than this linking verb? Have I used the correct form of the verb?" Model changing some words. On another reading, focus on adding adjectives to compare.

 TURN AND TALK Writers, how did using the sticky notes help me find places where I could change linking verbs to action verbs? Explain the difference between using -*er* and -*est* to compare. When do you use each?

 CREATE AUTHENTIC PURPOSES Have students look for pieces to revise in their own writing folders. They might identify verbs with sticky notes on a first reading and then reread to see if linking verbs could be replaced with action verbs. Encourage them to also look for places where adding a comparison could make the subject even clearer for readers.

 ASSESS THE LEARNING As students reread their pieces as editors, watch for those who may need extra support with verbs and comparative and superlative adjectives. Offer those students help individually or in small groups.

SUM IT UP Writers, we are becoming "master mechanics!" It takes a lot of skill to use verbs, and we are learning how to use many kinds of them. We know how to use adjectives to compare, too, and that helps create clear pictures in our readers' minds.

DAY 3 — Support and Extend the Learning

Select experiences that will best support your learners:

- Expand on the idea of content-area poems by having students write poetry from the point of view of a state, historical figure, an object, a concept in science or math, and so on. Encourage students to use poetic language, adjectives, and different types of verbs in their poems.

- Students can go on scavenger hunts to find both regular and irregular verbs in a piece of text. Encourage them to write the verbs they find on a T-chart or put them on sticky notes and add them to a large class T-chart.

- For students who have mastered regular forms of comparative and superlative adjectives, introduce irregular forms, such as *good, better, best* and *bad, worse,* and *worst*. Students can keep a list of irregular forms in their writing notebooks to use as a reference.

- Provide sentences that include linking verbs. Students can work individually or in pairs to replace the linking verbs with action verbs.

Pulling It All Together Cycle #7: Newsletter Article

Verb Tense • Transition Words • Homophones

DAY 1 **Model Writing for an Audience**

Each week, I send a newsletter to your parents. I am going to focus on what we've been learning about writing and editing as I draft an article. We've learned about verb tenses, using transition words, and noticing homophones. I want to be sure I do my best on these elements of writing. My first sentence is *During the last week, we start our unit on living things*. Notice how I used the transition word *during* to indicate time. I think my verb is a little off. I need to make it past tense and say, *started*. I also want to check the word *our*. I know this is a homophone. *Hour* (h-o-u-r) means the time; *our* (o-u-r) shows possession. I need to be careful. In my third sentence, I am shifting to tell what we will be doing later. *In a few weeks, we will study with an expert here...* Did you notice how I selected a transition phrase that suggests the future? Let's check the verbs to be sure they are future tense, too. I used the homophone *here*. Should it be *here* (h-e-r-e) or *hear* (h-e-a-r)? Let's reread to see how I did with verb tenses, transition words, and homophones.

> **Modeled Writing Sample**
>
> During the last week, we started our unit on Living Things. Acting as investigators, we researched various forms of plant life and development. In a few weeks, we will study with an expert here at school. The director of the arboretum is bringing exotic plants from all around the world.

 TURN AND TALK Talk with your partner. Reread once to check my verbs. Be sure I used the correct tense. Then reread to notice the transition words, and finally, reread for homophones. Share your observations.

 CREATE AUTHENTIC PURPOSE Let students know that they will work with partners to write a newsletter article about a classroom event or something they have learned. The audience is their parents. Encourage them to pay close attention to verb forms, transition words, and homophones.

✔️ **ASSESS THE LEARNING** As partners write their articles, check their work to identify students who might need extra assistance with verb tense.

🙂 **SUM IT UP** Writers, we had an important audience, and you stepped up to the challenge! You are becoming experts with verb tenses, transition words, and homophones. Your writing sounds more polished every day!

MODEL: APPLY THE LEARNING TO DAILY WRITING Model how to select a piece of writing from your writing folder and reread to check for verb tense, transition words and phrases followed by a comma, and homophones. As you identify these elements in the writing, think aloud and share your ideas about adjustments that you need to make.

 TURN AND TALK Writers, what did you see me do as I checked my writing? Talk about the verbs. How did I check for the correct form? How can we help ourselves remember to watch for homophones and to use terrific transition words or phrases?

 CREATE AUTHENTIC PURPOSES Have students look through their writing folders to find a piece of writing that might need a second look at verbs, transition words, or homophones. Have partners work together to identify the verbs in the sentences and then check them to be sure they "work." Remind students to ask themselves, "When did (or will) this action take place?"

 ASSESS THE LEARNING As partners work together to reread their writing, identify students who may need extra support with verbs or homophones. These students might benefit from reteaching the strategies in this cycle.

SUM IT UP The strategies you've learned help your writing make sense—not everything in our writing is taking place right now, so we need to use different verb tenses to show when things happened or will happen. Transition words and phrases, followed by a comma, can help us indicate time as well. They work together with verbs to help our readers understand when things are happening. Homophones, those tricky words that sound the same but have different spellings and meanings, keep us on our toes.

DAY 3 **Support and Extend the Learning**

Select experiences that will best support your learners:

• Encourage students to report on events in their town, at school, and around the globe. Then publish their articles in your class newsletter with a photo of the author.

• Provide sentences with present-tense verbs. Ask students to rewrite the sentences so the action takes place in the past and then in the future. Remind them that they may have to add helping verbs to some of the verbs. A pocket chart may be helpful for this experience.

• Have students engage in a scavenger hunt for terrific transitions or great context sentences for homophones. Post their examples.

• Have partners read through a science book and identify patterns of verb use. Do they tend to be present, past, or future tense? Repeat the survey with a social studies book. What do they notice now?

Pulling It All Together Cycle #8: Persuasive Letter

Apostrophe in Plural Possessive Nouns • Pronouns: Possessive • Pronouns: Subjective and Objective Cases

DAY 1 **Model Writing for an Audience**

We've been talking about eating healthy foods. I'm concerned about the contents in our vending machines, so I'm writing a persuasive letter to the school board. Persuasive writing tries to get people to think or believe something. I'm going to pay special attention to possessive nouns and to different kinds of pronouns. I am going to start with a strong statement: *We are concerned!* Now I'll state the problem. *Machines* is a plural noun. To make the possessive form, I don't add an apostrophe and *-s*, just an apostrophe. Let's look at the end of the next sentence: *Chips aren't good for we*. *We* is a pronoun that means more than one, but it's the wrong pronoun. *We* is used as the subject of a sentence, but this pronoun is after a preposition, so I need to use the objective case, *us*. I am starting my next sentence with *we*, because *we* is the pronoun used for a subject. In my last sentence, I have two possessive pronouns: *our* and *your*. I thought carefully about to whom I was referring—*our* refers to this group of students writing the letter, and *your* refers to the school board.

> **Modeled Writing Sample**
>
> Dear School Board,
>
> We are concerned! Our vending machines' contents are unhealthy. Cookies, candy, and potato chips aren't good for us. We would like to see them replaced with vegetables, cheese, and crackers. Healthier students learn better! Our health is in your hands.
>
> Sincerely,
>
> Mr. Arnold's class

 TURN AND TALK Writers, what are some things you noticed me doing while I wrote this letter? What kinds of pronouns did I use? How is *we* different from *our* and *us*? If I were talking about the contents of just one machine, how would that possessive look?

CREATE AUTHENTIC PURPOSE Have students work with partners or in groups to write a persuasive letter. Be sure that the letters have an audience, whether the audience is the school librarian, being asked to include more copies of a favorite book, or an elected official, being requested to take action on a topic like global warming.

ASSESS THE LEARNING As students craft their letters, circulate and use a class record-keeping grid to note students who are having difficulty using possessive forms of plural nouns and correct forms of pronouns. These students may benefit from small-group support.

SUM IT UP Writers, persuasive letters are important, because we want the reader to act on something that means a lot to us. Doing our best writing helps get that message across. We paid special attention to our pronouns and possessives to create powerful messages.

DAY 2 | Guided Practice

MODEL: APPLY THE LEARNING TO DAILY WRITING Review a previous modeled writing. Model how to check whether you have used the correct form of a pronoun by asking yourself if the pronoun is in the subject or object part of a sentence, or shows ownership. Insert a plural possessive noun that correctly uses an apostrophe after the *s*.

 TURN AND TALK Writers, what did you notice about the way that I checked to see if I used pronouns correctly? How can you use these strategies in your own editing? What did you see me doing that you could try yourself?

 CREATE AUTHENTIC PURPOSES Students look through their own writing folders to find pieces to revise. Encourage them to mark all the pronouns with sticky notes, then go back to check on the forms of the pronouns they used. Encourage them to include a plural possessive noun. Where should they place the apostrophe?

 ASSESS THE LEARNING As students reread their writing, confer with them to be sure they understand the differences between possessive, objective, and subjective pronouns. Look for the correct use of apostrophes in possessive nouns. Provide extra support as needed.

 SUM IT UP We are learning how to create powerful writing! We know that it's important to think about how we are using the pronoun before we choose the correct one. For plural possessive nouns, we show ownership by placing an apostrophe after the *-s*.

DAY 3 | Support and Extend the Learning

Select experiences that will best support your learners:

- Ask students to think of other authentic reasons to write persuasive letters. Expand the idea of persuasive writing into a debate by choosing a statement such as, *The school day should be extended by an hour each day.* One group can take the pro side of the argument, while the other takes the con. Encourage students to use facts to support their arguments.

- Give groups of students sentences that have nouns as both subjects and objects. Ask students to replace the nouns with the appropriate pronouns.

- Write possessive phrases, both singular and plural, on strips. Ask students to work in small groups to correctly place the apostrophe in each phrase. You might also have students change singular possessives into plural possessives.

- Students can hunt through texts to find examples of possessive nouns and then replace those possessive nouns with pronouns.

Pulling It All Together Cycle #9: Organizing Notes

Commas to Set Off Opener • Spelling Consciousness • Proofreading and Editing During and After Writing

DAY 1   Model Writing for an Audience

Taking notes helps you remember important information. It's a good idea to go back and organize and edit your notes to make sure they make sense. I am taking notes on states of matter. I'm thinking about spelling, and I'll edit during and after my note taking. We've been working on commas in sentences, so I'll pay attention to that, too. In my first sentence, I have a word that's hard for me to spell: *liquid*. I know there are different ways to make the sounds in the middle of the word. Is *liquid* spelled *l-i-k-w-i-d*? or *l-i-q-u-i-d*? I'll spell the word with a *qu*, but I'll put a small *sp* above it to remind me to check it later. I am going to organize my notes. There are three states of matter, so I'm going to use three bullets and underline each type. A solid does not change its shape. Should I use *it's* or *its*? *It's* means *it is*, and *its* is a possessive pronoun. I should use the possessive pronoun in this case. In the second bullet, I'm comparing solids and liquids. I start my second sentence with *unlike solids*, so I need to put a comma after the opener.

Modeled Writing Sample

Matter: Solid, Liquid, and Gas.

- A <u>solid</u> does not change its shape or size. Wood is a solid.

- A <u>liquid</u> has size or a volume, but not a definite shape. Unlike solids, liquids take the shape of their containers. Ice is a solid that becomes a liquid when it melts.

- <u>Gas</u> is matter that has no size, shape, or color of its own. Air is made of gases.

 TURN AND TALK Writers, talk about my notes. How are they organized? How will that help me find the information I need? How did I edit while I wrote? What else should I edit now?

CREATE AUTHENTIC PURPOSE Encourage students to take notes on a section of a content-area book. Each group can take notes on one section and share them with other students. Have students organize the notes while they are conscious of spelling, editing, and punctuation.

ASSESS THE LEARNING Use a class record-keeping grid to assess students' spelling consciousness, ability to edit during writing, and use commas in complex sentences. Plan to assist students in a small group or individual settings who need extra help.

SUM IT UP Taking notes helps you remember important information—but only if the notes make sense! That's why we revisit our notes and reorganize them. Writers, you pay careful attention to spelling and editing as you go, and you are putting commas in sentences to help them make sense. These strategies make your notes clear.

Guided Practice

MODEL: APPLY THE LEARNING TO DAILY WRITING Look through your previous modeled writing pieces to find informational writing. Consider the organization of the writing as you reread. Show how you "try out" spellings and then check them as you model editing as you go. Find a sentence that would benefit from an interesting opener and add both the opener and the comma.

 TURN AND TALK What did you see me do? What did you see me do to check spelling? How did adding an opener make my writing more interesting to read?

 CREATE AUTHENTIC PURPOSES Have students look through their own writing folders to find pieces to reread. Encourage them to use what they know about spelling and editing to create clear writing. Ask them to add one sentence opening to make their writing easier to understand.

 ASSESS THE LEARNING As students edit, check to see if they are paying attention to spelling and editing while they write and if they are using commas in sentence openers. Note which students need extra support with these strategies.

SUM IT UP Editing and organizing notes may seem like extra work, but when we edit our notes, we know we'll understand them later. Sentence openers give details that help us do things, like compare and contrast. Our editing skills will help us learn more and learn better.

DAY 3 Support and Extend the Learning

Select experiences that will best support your learners:

- Ask students to contribute to a list of spelling rules to post in the classroom. You might start with a published list of favorite mnemonics, but encourage students to contribute to the rules as they discover or devise new ones and to use the list as a reference.

- Encourage students to find and celebrate examples of strong sentence openers. They can read them aloud and write them on strips to post in the room for inspiration.

- Why proofread and edit during writing? Students can write notes to their families to explain what they've learned about writing and why editing during writing helps make their work more powerful. Why proofread and edit after writing?

- Invite students to choose pieces of writing from their folders that were made stronger during the proofreading and editing process. Encourage students to share with their learning partners what changes they made and how those changes made their writing more powerful. Partners can share celebrations of the work.

Pulling It All Together Cycle #10: Personal Narrative

End Punctuation of Four Kinds of Sentences • Portable Word Walls • Checklist for Focused Proofreading and Editing

DAY 1 Model Writing for an Audience

A personal narrative is a story about something that happened to the writer. I am going to write about something related to habitats. Not only will I think about my personal experience with habitats, I'll focus on editing strategies—end punctuation, portable word walls, and using a checklist for focused proofreading and editing. I'm writing about something that happened in my neighborhood. I saw a deer in our backyard. I start my writing with a strong, exciting statement—an exclamation. So I include an exclamation point. In the second sentence, I want to make sure I've spelled words correctly. *You* and *would* are both on my portable word wall, so I can double-check them as I go. Once I finish, I am going to proofread and edit with my checklist. I reread for one editing point at a time rather than all of them at once. This helps me identify errors and, more important, fix them!

Modeled Writing Sample

I couldn't believe my eyes! You would never expect to see this in a crowded city. A deer was standing in my backyard, munching on the grass. I was worried that it would get hit by a car if it tried to leave the yard. We called animal rescue, and they planned to release it in a forest. I asked the worker, "Are people moving too close to animal habitats?"

TURN AND TALK Writers, what did you notice while I was writing this narrative? Find a sentence with a question mark. Why does that sentence need the question mark? Talk about my editing. Why is it helpful to check for one focus on each reading?

CREATE AUTHENTIC PURPOSE Have students write their own personal narratives. Remind them that a narrative is a story that is based on a personal experience. Students should pay special attention to end punctuation and proofread and edit with portable word walls and their editing checklists. To make the writing more authentic, plan to compile student writing in a book, enter them in competitions, and so on.

ASSESS THE LEARNING Take time to observe or confer with students about their work. Do students know how to choose the correct end punctuation depending on the type of sentence? Can they proofread and edit with a portable word wall and a checklist? Provide support for students who need assistance.

SUM IT UP Sharing personal narratives can be fun, especially when we bring our stories to life with great writing! Portable word walls and editing checklists are tools to help your writing. Paying special attention to sentences and varying them is another strategy for making your writing clear and interesting.

DAY 2   Guided Practice

MODEL: APPLY THE LEARNING TO DAILY WRITING Find a piece of modeled writing to share with the class. Identify a place where you could turn a statement into a question or an exclamation to vary and liven up the writing. Model choosing the correct punctuation for a sentence. Show how you use both the word wall and an editing checklist to guide the editing process.

 TURN AND TALK Editors, turn and talk about how I used the word wall and the editing checklist. How did these tools help my proofreading and editing? Share one tip with your partner that will help him or her use these tools effectively.

 CREATE AUTHENTIC PURPOSES Ask students to find personal narratives in their own writing folders. Have partners see if they can identify places that might benefit from the addition of a question or exclamation, then trade papers and use word walls and editing checklists to guide their proofreading and editing work.

 ASSESS THE LEARNING As students reread their writing, use a class record-keeping grid to assess which students may need assistance with utilizing portable word walls and editing checklists or further help in punctuation.

 SUM IT UP I liked how all of you thought about varying your sentences and considered how to punctuate those sentences properly. I also appreciated the way you used two helpful tools—a word wall and an editing checklist—to strengthen your writing.

DAY 3   Support and Extend the Learning

Select experiences that will best support your learners::

- Provide a prompt for a personal narrative, and then allow students to draw comic strips to illustrate their stories. Then, have them write a sentence for each panel of the comic strip. Encourage them to use different types of sentences with correct punctuation.

- Have students meet in groups to create riddles about the sentence types—assign one sentence type to each group. Other groups guess the sentence type based on the riddle, such as *I am a sentence that tells you to clean up your room* (imperative) or *I am a sentence that shows inquiry* (question).

- Provide many opportunities for students to use editing checklists, both during and after writing. Editing checklists are more powerful when students create them because of the discussions they elicit about what makes strong writing even stronger.

Pulling It All Together Cycle #11: Summarizing Interviews

Commas to Set Off Closer • Pronouns: Subjective and Objective Cases • Punctuation in Direct Quotations (Dialogue)

DAY 1 Model Writing for an Audience

Interviewing is a wonderful way to learn firsthand about someone's life. I interviewed Mrs. Allen, our school cook, and will be writing about my interview. I will open with a quote. *"I grew up in southern Alabama with a mother who loved to cook,"* she smiled. Did you notice I used quotation marks around the words the speaker actually said to me? My next sentence is *These words were spoken softly by Mrs. Allen, our own very talented cook.* I used a closer and there is my comma. Hooray for me! *Nodding and leaning close, she confided that she doesn't use cookbooks.* I need to think about the pronoun *she*. *She* is replacing *Mrs. Allen*, my subject, so it needs to be subjective case. Let's look at the chart and see if I chose the correct pronoun. Writers, reread and check my summary.

> ### Modeled Writing Sample
>
> "I grew up in southern Alabama with a mother who loved to cook," she smiled. These words were spoken softly by Mrs. Allen, our own very talented cook. Nodding and leaning close, she confided that she doesn't use cookbooks! Now, that's a surprise.

TURN AND TALK Writers, think together about the punctuation of the dialogue, the comma and the closer, along with the subjective pronoun. Did I use what we have learned?

CREATE AUTHENTIC PURPOSE Have students work individually or in pairs to plan interview questions they could ask of someone at the school. Then send them off to their interviews with a clear understanding that they must include at least one direct quote. It would be ideal if the interviewers could take a picture of their subject to include with their published writing. Explain that after they complete the interview, they are to work as a team to write a summary that includes correct punctuation for dialogue, at least one closer with a comma, and pronouns for subjective/objective case.

ASSESS THE LEARNING As students work, use a class record-keeping grid to note students who may need additional help with the mechanics in this cycle. Meet with individuals or small groups to provide the extra support they need to master the strategies.

 SUM IT UP You have written wonderful summaries of your interviews. You understand the process now! You designed questions, collected information, and used lots of great editing strategies.

MODEL: APPLY THE LEARNING TO DAILY WRITING Choose a piece of writing from your modeled writing folder to edit with a careful eye toward pronouns, closers, and dialogue. Show students how you mark each of the pronouns with a sticky note. Think aloud about several of them, asking yourself if you should use objective or subjective case pronouns. Find a place to add a bit of dialogue and a closer.

 TURN AND TALK Writers, where in my writing could I add some dialogue? How would the addition of dialogue make the story more exciting or interesting? Where could I insert a closer?

 CREATE AUTHENTIC PURPOSES Ask students to turn to their writing folders to find pieces to reread, then use sticky notes to mark pronouns that they can revisit to check for the correct case. Encourage them to add a piece of dialogue and a closer to the writing to make it livelier and more exact. If necessary, remind them of punctuation rules.

 ASSESS THE LEARNING As students reread their writing, note which students are still having difficulty using the correct case of pronouns and properly punctuating closers and dialogue. Gather small groups for reteaching these points of mechanics.

SUM IT UP Writers, your eyes are getting sharper, and your ears are thinking of good spots to add dialogue and closers that will enliven the writing. You are properly punctuating these elements, and you know how to choose the correct pronouns. You should be proud of using these tools in your writing!

DAY 3 **Support and Extend the Learning**

Select experiences that will best support your learners:

- Provide students with scripts for plays or Readers Theater. Ask students how the dialogue is represented on the page. (Usually, the speaker's name comes at the beginning of the sentence, followed by a colon and the spoken words.) Students can rewrite parts of the script as dialogue, with commas and quotation marks.

- Write "secret sentences" with students. (See page 121.) Be sure that the secret sentences have closers. Check to be sure that students use commas to set off the closers as they physically arrange themselves and their words.

- On large sentence strips, write sentences that include nouns as subjects and objects. Give students sticky notes with subject and object pronouns. Students can place their sticky notes to correspond to the nouns in the sentences.

- Review favorite literature for dialogue and present it as Readers Theater, dramatically!

Pulling It All Together Cycle #12: Advice Letter

Subject-Verb Agreement for Plural Nouns and Pronouns • Apostrophe in Plural Possessive Nouns • Pronouns: Possessive

---

DAY 1 **Model Writing for an Audience**

We are almost done with fifth grade, and we have learned a lot this year. Today, we are going to write letters of advice to next year's fifth graders. I want to write good advice, but I also want to focus on some of our editing points: subject-verb agreement and possessive nouns and possessive pronouns. First, I write a greeting. In the next sentence, I start with the pronoun *we*. What verb should I use? *We* is plural, so I use a plural verb to agree—*want*, not *wants*. This part of my next sentence sounds a little awkward—*success will belong to you*. Hmmm... it would work better to use the possessive pronoun and write *success will be yours*. Much more natural! The next sentence has another plural noun as its subject—*lunch lines*. I need to make the verb agree again and use the word *move*, not *moves*. I'm puzzled by what to do in this sentence: *It's important for new students to listen to teachers' messages*. Those are messages from all the teachers, so I need to keep *teachers* plural. How do I make that word possessive? I add an apostrophe after the *-s*.

> **Modeled Writing Sample**
>
> Dear incoming students,
>
> We want you to succeed in fifth grade. Follow our tips, and success will be yours! The lunch lines move slowly. Bring your lunch so you can spend more time with your friends. Teachers' messages are important. Remember to listen, because they care about your success, too. Keep your desk and materials organized. Good luck in fifth grade!

👀 **TURN AND TALK** Writers, how did I show possession with a pronoun? With a plural noun? Explain how these are different. Find a plural subject and identify the verb. How would the verb change if the subject were singular?

✏️ **CREATE AUTHENTIC PURPOSE** Students can work in pairs or small groups to write letters of advice for incoming students. Remind them to pay careful attention to possessives and to subject–verb agreement, looking for both plural nouns and pronouns.

✅ **ASSESS THE LEARNING** As students work, note on a class record-keeping grid which students might need additional assistance in using possessive forms of plural nouns and plural pronouns. Do students make sure that their subjects and verbs agree in number? Be sure to provide support for students who need assistance.

 SUM IT UP Your advice letters will definitely help new students! The attention that you paid to subjects and verbs and to your possessives makes your message clear and easy to read.

DAY 2 Guided Practice

MODEL: APPLY THE LEARNING TO DAILY WRITING Revisit your modeled writing to find a piece that you can reread, looking carefully at subject-verb agreement and at possessives. Model "testing" the verb, for example: *The subject of this sentence is* students. *That word refers to more than one, so I need to use a plural verb. What if the subject were* student?

 TURN AND TALK Writers, what did you notice about the subjects and the verbs in my writing? How did I make sure they agree? What is the difference between a singular possessive and a plural possessive?

 CREATE AUTHENTIC PURPOSES Invite students to reread pieces from their own writing folders. Challenge them to change a plural possessive noun into a plural possessive pronoun. Have them underline subjects, identify them as singular or plural, and then check the verb for agreement.

 ASSESS THE LEARNING As students reread their writing, use your class record-keeping grid to track the progress of your students in using the mechanics in this cycle. Determine how you might help these students and support them in small-group or individual instruction.

😊 **SUM IT UP** Writers, you understand how important mechanics are in making writing not only interesting, but easy to read. Your messages are much more powerful! Plural possessive nouns and pronouns are formed differently than singular ones—you have that all figured out! Your subjects and verbs agree, helping you craft sentences that make sense.

DAY 3 Support and Extend the Learning

Select experiences that will best support your learners:

- Students will enjoy writing advice letters for incoming students. They may also want to write additional advice letters, for example, to favorite story characters, to their younger siblings, and so on.

- Give students sentences with singular nouns or pronouns as subjects. Students can replace the nouns or pronouns with their plural counterparts and then change the verbs to create correct sentences.

- Provide sentences in which phrases could be replaced by possessive pronouns. Encourage students to rewrite the sentences. Examples:

    The robins' home is a nest. The nest is theirs.

    Mom's purse is the red one. The red purse is hers.

    Dad's car needs repairs. The broken car is his.

PART IV

Tools

The tools presented in this section are designed to be time-savers to support you and your students in creating resources that empower your work as writers.

The Portable Word Wall on page 151 contains many high-frequency words, making it an especially important resource that can serve as a well from which you can draw words for spelling instruction, words for your word walls, and so on. These are the words students need most! Use this list to power-up your thinking and help you teach with maximum efficiency.

Please also take special notice of the Create Your Own Resource pages. These are designed to support students in creating references they can save and use over the course of the entire year. With sample sentences from mentor books and exemplars they create themselves, learners will have tools that will support and lift the writing they produce. We encourage you to have your students save the resources they create in their writing folders or writing notebooks for easy reference.

Contents

To print out the reproducibles on the following pages at full size, please visit: www.scholastic.com/masteringthemechanics.

Spelling Reference: Portable Word Wall

Name _____   * = Check *Tricky Words* Reference

A	C	G	J	N	R	U
a	called	gave	jump	name	ran	under
about	came	get	just	never	read	until
add	can	girl		new	ready	up
after	can't	give	**K**	next	really	us
again	children	go	kids	no*	right	use
all	city	going	kitten	not	run	
also	come	good	know*	now		**V**
always	could	got		numbers	**S**	very
an		grade	**L**		said	
and	**D**	great	last	**O**	same	**W**
another	dad		learned	of	saw	want
any	day	**H**	left	off	say	was
are*	dear	had	let	often	school	we
around	did	happy	like	old	see	were
as	didn't	has	lillle	on	set*	what
asked	do	have	live	once	she	when*
at	does	he	long	one	should	where
away	don't	hear	look	only	shouldn't	which
	down	help	looked	or	small	while
B		her	looking	other	so	who
back	**E**	here	love	our*	some	why
be	each	him		over	story	would
because	even	his	**M**	own	such	will
been	every	home	mad		sure	with
before		how	made	**P**		
best	**F**	however	make	page	**T**	**XYZ**
big	family		man	paper	take	yes
boy	father	**I**	many	people	tell	you
brother	find	I	math	place	than*	your*
but	first	I'll	me	plant	that	you're*
by*	for*	I'm	men	play	the	
	found	if	mother	put	their*	
	friend	if	much	putting	them	
	from	in	must		then*	
		into	my	**Q**	there*	
		is		question	they	
		isn't		quiet	they're*	
		it			this	
		its*			to*	
		it's*			today	

Spelling Reference: Tricky Words and Homophones

> Create sample mentor sentences in your writer's notebook for easy reference.

Writer/Researcher _____ Date _____

Writers need to be especially careful to use homophones correctly or their reader will be confused. These context sentences are examples to help you get started in creating your own list of sentences for homophones and other tricky words. Use a highlighter to identify words in column one that are homophones. Create some sample mentor sentences in your writer's notebook for easy reference.

Some Examples	Function/Purpose	Examples
are our hour	Are is a verb. Our is a possessive pronoun. Hour is a term showing time.	Are you going to help? This is our house. The parade starts in one hour.
buy by bye	Buy means "to purchase." By means "beside or near." Bye is a word to say when you're leaving.	Buy yourself a cool bike helmet. He walked right by me. The toddler waved, "Bye."
its it's	Its is a possessive pronoun. It's, a contraction, means "it is."	The bike spun its tires. It's a gorgeous day!
know no	Know means "to understand." No, an interjection, means "no."	It's helpful to know your address. No, I don't want to go.
lay lie	Lay means to put or to place. (lay, laid, laid) Lie means to recline. (lie, lay, lain) Lie means to tell a falsehood. (lie, lied, lied)	Lay it down on the table. Go lie down and take a nap. Don't lie. Please tell the truth.
lets let's	Lets means "allowed." Let's, a contraction, means "let us."	Mom lets us drink juice. Let's go to the park!
right write	Right means to be correct or indicates a direction such as the right vs. left side. Write means to put something in print.	Your answer is right. Turn right at the corner. I'll write my phone number for you.
set sit	Set means "to put something someplace." Sit means "to rest on a seat."	Set the apple on the plate. Sit in the first seat.
than then	Than is used when comparing two things. Then, an adverb, indicates a particular time.	She is taller than you. Eat your lunch, then go to recess.
their there they're	Their means "belonging to them." There means "at or in that place." They're, a contraction, means "they are."	Their backyard is huge! Put the book over there. They're going to the library.
to too two	To means "toward." Too means "also" or "more than needed." Two is a number.	They're going to the museum. I ate way too much. We have two spotted puppies.
your you're	Your is a possessive pronoun. You're, a contraction, means "you are."	Your hair is a cool color! You're my best friend.

Other tricky words and homophones to consider: allowed, aloud; ate, eight; aisle, I'll; billed, build; blue, blew; bored, board; creak, creek; ceiling, sealing; chili, chilly; days, daze; dear, deer; doe, dough; discussed, disgust; eight, ate; fair, fare; guest, guessed; here, hear; hole, whole; knead, need; knew, new; knot, not; made, maid; one, won; pear, pair; sea, see; some, sum; son, sun; way, weigh; wait, weight; wood, would.

© 2008 Hoyt & Therriault • Scholastic • *Mastering the Mechanics: Grades 4–5*

Create Your Own Resource: Using "ing" Words and Commas

Writer/Researcher _____ Date _____

Commas and "ing" words make terrific partners. They can help you write sentences that are creative, interesting, and filled with strong images for your reader. Adding action, images, and sounds to your sentences with "ing" words and commas makes them come alive!

Mentor Sentences: "ing" phrases <u>followed</u> by a comma

> <u>Dragging</u> his feet and hanging his head, Andrew slowly approached his furious mother.
>
> <u>Barking</u> ferociously, the dog raced toward the cat.

You try it!

_____

_____

Find an "ing" phrase followed by a comma in a mentor book.

The sentence I found: _____

I found this in _____ (name of book) by

_____ on page _____.

Mentor Sentence: Comma <u>before</u> "ing" phrases

> Andrew slowly approached his furious mother, <u>dragging</u> his feet and hanging his head.
>
> The dog raced toward the cat, <u>barking</u> ferociously.

You try it!

_____

_____

Find a comma before an "ing" phrase in a mentor book.

The sentence I found: _____

I found this in _____ (name of book) by

_____ on page _____.

© 2008 Hoyt & Therriault • Scholastic • *Mastering the Mechanics: Grades 4–5*

Create Your Own Resource: Combining Sentences With a Comma and a Linking Word

Writer/Researcher _____ Date _____

Commas and linking words can help us turn short, choppy sentences into more interesting structures. These tools can help us create sentences that flow smoothly and sound more natural. Linking words often used include *and, but, for, or, yet, so*.

Separate Sentences	Mentor Sentence
The dog barked. The cat raced toward the house.	The dog barked, <u>and</u> the cat raced toward the house.
I did my homework. I forgot it at home.	I did my homework, <u>but</u> I forgot it at home.

You try it!
Search mentor books to find a long sentence that is really two short sentences joined by a linking word and a comma.

The sentence I found: _____

I found this in _____ (name of book) on page _____. The linking

word is _____. If this had been written as two separate sentences, it might have looked like:

Sentence 1: _____

Sentence 2: _____

Find Another One!
Search mentor books to find a long sentence that is really two short sentences joined by a linking word and a comma.

The sentence I found: _____

I found this in _____ (name of book) on page _____. The linking

word is _____. If this had been written as two separate sentences, it might have looked like:

Sentence 1: _____

Sentence 2: _____

What have you learned about creating longer, more natural sentences out of short sentences?

_____

_____

Create Your Own Resource: Transition Words

Writer/Researcher _____ Date _____

Transition words create connections between ideas and cue the reader about important information.

Purpose	Example of Transition Words
Time/sequence (the order in which something happens)	first, second, third, before, during, after, today, tomorrow, yesterday, until, next, then, as soon as, finally, afterward, earlier, meanwhile, now, since, soon
Show place	above, across, against, along, adjacent to, beyond, by, down, on the opposite side, nearby, to the left of
Compare/contrast (show differences)	however, but, although, on the other hand, similarly, even though, still, though, yet, also, likewise
Conclude, summarize or emphasize a point (the end of the writing is coming)	finally, in conclusion, therefore, in other words, in summary, last
Add information	first, also, and, besides, in addition, for example, next, finally, for instance, specifically, in fact, of course, to illustrate, for instance
Example or illustration	Specifically, for example, in fact, of course, to illustrate, for instance

Transition words I found

They were located in (book)

The author's purpose in using them was to ....

_____   _____   _____

_____   _____   _____

_____   _____   _____

_____   _____   _____

Create Your Own Resource: Identifying Verb Types

Writer/Researcher _____ Date _____

Review your favorite books for examples of different kinds of verbs

Action Verbs (These are the engines of sentences)

_____ _____ _____ _____

Linking Verbs

_____ _____ _____ _____

Helping Verbs

_____ _____ _____ _____

My favorite mentor books for finding great verbs are: _____

A verb shows action or links the subject to another word in the sentence.

Action Verbs

An **action verb** tells what the subject is doing. Some experts think that the verb is the most important part of speech. They make writing specific and clear.

EXAMPLE: Ice cream *dribbled* down his chin. The worm *slithered* through the grass.

Linking Verbs

A **linking verb** links a subject to a noun or an adjective that comes after the verb.

EXAMPLE: My puppy *is* sweet.

Linking verbs ("be" verbs): is, are, was, were, am, been

EXAMPLE: The painting *looks* strange. (Paintings don't see! Looks doesn't show action in this sentence. This sentence means the painting is strange.)

Other linking verbs: feel, look, remain, seem, smell, sound, taste (These words can be action words, too.)

Helping Verbs

Helping verbs come before the main verb and they help state the action or show when the action is taking place.

EXAMPLE: I *will* eat my breakfast. (The verb *will* helps tell about a future action, *will eat*.)

EXAMPLE: We *have been* waiting patiently. (The verbs *have been* help tell that an action is still happening, *have been waiting*.)

Helping verbs: is, are, was, were, am, been, have, had, has, do, did, can, will, could, would, should, must, may, shall.

When the verb is composed of two or more words, it is called a **verb phrase**.

Create Your Own Resource: Understanding Adverbs and Prepositional Phrases

Writer/Researcher _____ Date _____

An **adverb** tells where (here, there), when (now, later), how (slowly, quickly), and to what degree (very, slightly). An adverb often ends in –ly.

A **preposition** is a word that relates a noun or pronoun to another word in the sentence. (*She placed the book _on_ the round table.*)

A **prepositional phrase** is a group of words that include a preposition, its object, and any describing words that come in between. (*She placed the book _on the round table_*).

Common Prepositions and Phrases

> about, above, across, after, against, along, among, around, at, before, behind, below, beneath, beside, between, by, down, during, except, for, from, in, in front of, inside, instead of, into, like, near, of off, on, on top of, out of, outside, over, since, through, to, toward, under, underneath, until, up, upon, with, within, without

Writers, grab a stack of your favorite books and start searching for adverbs and prepositional phrases. Notice how your favorite authors use adverbs and prepositional phrases to provide readers with strong images.

• Highlight the prepositions above that you found most often in the books you reviewed.

• Which of the authors seemed to use them the most?

Write your favorite sentences that include adverbs or prepositional phrases below, and include where you found them.

_____ (sentence)

_____ (book)

_____ (sentence)

_____ (book)

_____ (sentence)

_____ (book)

• What did you notice about adverbs and prepositions in the books you reviewed?

• After you collect some great examples, challenge yourselves to enliven your own writing with adverbs and prepositional phrases.

> ### See why writers simply ADORE THESE WORDS!
>
> <u>With</u> grins on our faces, my friends and I stood at the edge of the pool. <u>Without</u> saying a word, we grabbed hands and blasted into the cool, crisp water. <u>Around</u> the edges, <u>through</u> the middle, and <u>across</u> the thrashing waves, we played like agile porpoises…
>
> A challenge. Review your writing and find places where you can liven up sentences by beginning with a preposition!

A Guide to Common Irregular Verbs

Writer/Researcher _____ Date _____

Watch for these verb forms when you are reading. When you see one in print or use it in your own writing, place a tally mark next to the word and tell where you found it.

Present Tense	Past Tense	Tally	Where I saw it or where I used it	Present Tense	Past Tense	Tally	Where I saw it or where I used it
am	was, were			lose	lost		
begin	began			ride	rode		
bite	bit			rise	rose		
break	broke			run	ran		
bring	brought			say	said		
catch	caught			see	saw		
come	came			send	sent		
dive	dove, dived			set	set		
do	did			shake	shook		
draw	drew			shrink	shrank		
drink	drank			sing	sang		
drive	drove			sit	sat		
eat	ate			speak	spoke		
fall	fell			steal	stole		
fly	flew			swim	swam		
forget	forgot			take	took		
get	got			teach	taught		
give	gave			tear	tore		
go	went			tell	told		
grow	grew			think	thought		
hide	hid			throw	threw		
know	knew			understand	understood		
lay (place)	laid			wake	woke, waked		
leave	left			wear	wore		
let	let			write	wrote		
lie (recline)	lay						

Understanding the Parts of Speech

Writer/Researcher _____ Date _____

The English language has thousands of words, but they can all be divided into eight groups called the *parts of speech*.

Writers, after learning about each *part of speech*, include your own examples:

1. **Nouns:** name a person, place, thing, or idea (*child, Carol, lake, book, honesty*)

   _____

2. **Pronouns:** take the place of nouns (*I, me, you, she, he, we, you, they, us*)

   _____

3. **Verbs:** express action or state of being (*skip, read, is, are, was helping*)

   _____

4. **Adjectives:** describe a noun or a pronoun (*awesome, fantastic, cool*)

   _____

5. **Interjections:** express strong emotion or surprise
   (*Whoa! Look out!*) (*Whoa, look out!*)

   _____

6. **Connecting words:** connect words, groups of words, or sentences
   (*and, or, because*)

   _____

7. **Adverbs and adverb phrases:** tell when, how, and to what degree.
   (describe a verb, an adjective, or another adverb)
   (*on the roof, quickly, at high noon*)

   _____

8. **Prepositions:** relate nouns or pronouns to another word in a sentence
   (<u>on</u> the steep roof, <u>in</u> the hidden box, <u>under</u> the low table, <u>to</u> the store)

   _____

© 2008 Hoyt & Therriault • Scholastic • *Mastering the Mechanics: Grades 4–5*

Copy Editor's Symbols

ዋ	Take it out.	I'm a g~~q~~ood writer.
∧	Put something in.	good I'm a ∧ writer.
∧ ＃	Put in space.	I'm agood writer. ∧ ＃
⊙	Add a period.	I'm a good writer⊙
＝	Make this a capital letter.	i'm a good writer. ＝
/	Make this capital letter lowercase.	I'm a Ǥood writer.
sp	Spelling error.	I'm a good (writter.) sp

From the Desk of

_____

From the Desk of

_____

From the Desk of

_____

From the Desk of

_____

Interest Inventory

Name _____ Date _____

Date of birth _____ Number of siblings _____

Siblings' names: _____

	Your favorite	Your least favorite
pet		
color		
food		
beverage		
restaurant		
subject		
book title		
author		
sport		
sports team		
theme park		
actor/athlete		
other		

Where have you lived?

City and state_____

Hobbies/interests: _____

List important qualities in a friend: _____

_____

Write whatever you would like to add: _____

_____

_____

© 2008 Hoyt & Therriault • Scholastic • *Mastering the Mechanics: Grades 4–5*

Yearlong Planner

Consider: Are there any lessons that should appear multiple times?

	September	October	November	December	January	February	March	April	May	June
WEEK 1										
WEEK 2										
WEEK 3										
WEEK 4										

PART V

Assessment and Record Keeping

The assessment tools and record-keeping sheets in this section are designed as suggestions. You may find that some match perfectly the needs of your students or your personal preferences in record keeping. We encourage you to make these tools your own or use them as springboards for the creation of tools that are just right for you and your learners.

We have deliberately tried to highlight several kinds of assessments for your consideration. You will notice that there are student self-reflections in the form of editing checklists, spelling self-reflections, and "Skills I Can Use." There are cloze experiences to assess proficiency with pronouns and verbs, which we encourage you to use as models in creating your own cloze experiences focused on any number of conventions and mechanics. There are also several class-planning grids designed to support your observation of learners, create small groups with similar needs, and to assist you as you coach writers during one-on-one conferences.

Most of all, select the tools that will empower you to watch your students closely. Observations and ongoing daily assessments give power to instruction and enable you to respond to the needs of individuals and gather small groups with similar needs or select from available resources. You are the driving force in instruction. You are the only one who truly sees your students as individuals and can select supports that will lift their learning.

To print out the reproducibles on the following pages at full size, please visit: www.scholastic.com/masteringthemechanics.

Contents

Editing Checklist I

Author _____ Peer Editor _____ Date _____

We have reviewed this work to check for:

SPELLING
❑ Misspelled words

CAPITALIZATION
❑ Proper Names
❑ Proper Adjectives
❑ Titles
❑ Headings

PUNCTUATION
❑ End of sentence (. ? !)
❑ Comma after opener
❑ Comma before closer

GRAMMAR
❑ Complete sentences, not fragments

Editing Checklist II

Author _____ Peer Editor _____ Date _____

We have reviewed this work to check for:

SPELLING
❑ We corrected spelling on: _____, _____, _____
❑ We checked the tricky word list, including homophones
❑ Resources that helped us check spelling include: _____

CAPITALIZATION
❑ Beginning of sentence
❑ Proper nouns, proper adjectives (English muffin)

PUNCTUATION
❑ End of sentence (. ? !)
❑ Sentence opener followed by a comma
❑ Compound sentence joined by a linking word and a comma

GRAMMAR
❑ Complete sentences (Who/what did something? What did they do?)
❑ No fragments
❑ Some interesting sentences:

The most interesting sentence in this piece is _____

_____.

We think this sentence is strong because _____

_____.

Editing Checklist III

Author _____ Peer Editor _____ Date _____

We have reviewed this work to check for:

SPELLING

Resources we used to correct spelling include:

_____

❏ Three words we corrected:

_____, _____, _____

❏ We checked the tricky word list, including homophones

❏ Every syllable was checked to be sure there was a vowel

❏ Homophones are used correctly

PUNCTUATION

❏ End of sentence (. ? !)

❏ Apostrophe for possessive

❏ Sentence openers are followed by a comma

❏ Commas separate items in a series

❏ Compound sentences are joined by a linking word and a comma

❏ Exclamation point for interjection

❏ Items in a series are joined by commas

❏ Dialogue is inserted and correctly punctuated

GRAMMAR

❏ Complete sentence (Who/what did something? What did they do?)

❏ This piece is free of fragments

❏ This piece has no run-on sentences; the word *and* is used sparingly

❏ There are no double subjects (*My mom she*)

❏ There is subject-verb agreement in all sentences

❏ Verb tenses are correctly used

❏ Transition words and phrases link ideas and show passage of time

❏ Pronoun order is correct (*My mom and I*)

❏ Pronouns clearly refer to their antecedents

❏ Verbs are carefully selected to serve as engines of sentence

Editing Checklist IV: Focus on Grammar

Author _____ Peer Editor _____ Date _____

We have reviewed this work to check for:

VERBS

❏ Verb tense is consistent throughout (all past tense or all present tense)

❏ Verb case is correct: *We saw a plane* vs. *We seen a plane*

❏ Verbs are strong and show action

PRONOUNS

❏ The reader can clearly tell which noun a pronoun refers to (*antecedent*)

❏ Pronouns clearly show gender and number (*he, she, they, we*)

❏ Possessive pronouns are used correctly (*his, hers, ours, theirs*)

SENTENCE

❏ Each sentence is complete; there are no fragments

❏ There are no double subjects (My mom, she…)

❏ There are no double negatives (We don't got no…)

❏ Subjects and verbs agree (singular and plural)

❏ Adverbs, adverb phrases, and prepositional phrases are used as openers to some sentences

Our favorite grammatically correct sentence is

_____.

We picked this because _____

_____.

Spelling Strategies Self-Assessment

Writer_____ Date _____

During drafting, when I come to a word I am not sure of, I usually _____

or _____. During editing, I would follow up on the word by _____

_____ or _____.

Mark the strategies you use: (Put a star next to the ones you use the most)

❑ Stretch words out slowly and listen to sounds

❑ Draw a line under words I am not sure of during drafting or write *sp.*

❑ Tap out the syllables and check each syllable for a vowel

❑ Try to visualize what the word looks like

❑ Use another piece of paper or the margin to spell the word several ways

❑ Use words I know to spell other words

❑ Use a portable word wall

❑ Use the class word wall

❑ Refer to the tricky words and homophone lists

❑ Use a dictionary

❑ Use a thesaurus

❑ If I know I can find the word quickly, I might _____.

❑ If I think it will take me some time to find the correct spelling, I wait until editing, then I

_____

❑ During proofreading and editing, I ask a friend to edit with me

❑ During proofreading and editing, I add words to my portable word wall that I think I will use again

If I were to give advice to a younger student about spelling, I would tell that writer:

_____

_____

Interactive Assessment

Focus on capitalization, spelling, punctuation, grammar, spacing or editing

Date _____ Title of Writing _____ Author_____

Dear Parent/Guardian,

Thank you for joining our celebration of your child's writing. Please add your response and return this form and the writing to school tomorrow.

The Author

As I look at this writing and editing, I am especially proud of _____

_____

_____

_____

_____

Author _____

The Teacher

As I look at this writing and editing, I am especially proud of _____

_____

_____

_____

_____

Teacher _____

Through the Eyes of a Parent

As I look at this writing and editing, I am especially proud of _____

_____

_____

_____

_____

Parent _____

Skills I Can Use

Name _____

Skill used in my writing	I took control of this skill on (date) _____

The Heart

With unrelenting consistency, the muscles of the heart _____ together. These contractions of the heart are so powerful that they could _____ a jet of water six feet into the air. Each time the muscles contract, blood _____ through the chambers of the heart, gathering speed, _____ and _____ with power. As the blood _____ out of the left ventricle of the heart, it _____ with great force into the aorta, the blood vessel that _____ blood away from the heart and toward the rest of the body. Deep and fast, blood _____ into ever-smaller tunnels. Shivery and quick, blood _____ into veins and capillaries, _____ oxygen and nutrients to needy cells.

Note to teacher: Place this selection on the overhead or provide copies for partners. Partners think together to identify action words that would complete the blanks. A few suggestions to get you going:

squeeze, work, flow, blast, shoot, surges, pushes, pulsing, pushing, racing

Assessment Tool: Identifying Pronouns and Their Antecedents

Tracks

The Kroger kids lived on a remote homestead and walked several miles each day to get to and from school. Since the trip was so long, they often stopped to rest near a gorgeous waterfall. While resting one day, Andrew, the oldest, started making mountain lion tracks in the soft dirt. He used his knuckles and a stick, creating tracks that looked quite real. Then, he got the bright idea to have his little brother and sister leave their footprints with the mountain lion "tracks" right behind them. They thought it was great fun and continued leaving their tracks all the way to town.

When they left school that day, the kids were shocked to see that the town was in an uproar. Men had left their homesteads and were gathering with guns and horses. A rancher had spotted mountain lion tracks that appeared to have followed small children right into town. The men of the town were organizing a hunting party and gathering bloodhounds to track down the mountain lion so children would not be in danger.

Note to teacher: Place this passage on the overhead and show your students how to:
1. Underline pronouns in the first paragraph
2. Identify the antecedent for each pronoun and draw a line from the pronoun to the antecedent.
3. Work together to identify pronouns and antecedents for the second paragraph.

Assessment Tool: Cloze for Subject-Verb Agreement, Verb Tense, and Punctuation

The Artistic Elephant: A True Story

Elephants _____ widely known to be well suited to training_ At a circus_ I once _____ an elephant lift a telephone pole in its trunk while carrying a passenger on its back_ But that is nothing compared to this true story_

In the early 1970s_ an elephant named Ruby _____ transported from a working lumber camp in Thailand to the zoo in Phoenix_ Arizona_ At the camp_ she _____ kept busy with hard work_ but at the zoo she was bored_ Ruby started chasing the zookeepers and bothering the other animals_ The zookeepers _____ frustrated and didn't know what to do_

A creative trainer realized she could _____ her trunk to hold a paintbrush dabbed in paint_ She then _____ to rub the brush on a canvas_ creating pictures. Ruby _____ to select colors from a palate and was soon drawing attention from newspaper reporters and magazines writers_

The trainer did not intend to draw attention to Ruby_s art. He was just trying to keep her busy_

But we must wonder… Painting is not natural for elephants_ so is this the right thing to do_ What is wrong in a zoo if animals are bored_ If we were to critically analyze this situation, what do we think should happen_

Hints to get you started

is, are

saw, seen

is, was, were

is, was, were

was, were

© 2008 Hoyt & Therriault • Scholastic • *Mastering the Mechanics: Grades 4–5*

Note to teacher: Place this selection on the overhead or provide copies for partners. Their task is to insert appropriate words and punctuation marks, keeping in mind what they know about subject-verb agreement, verb tense, and punctuation.

Class Record-Keeping Grid

Class Record-Keeping Grid: Capitalization

	Proper nouns: people	Proper nouns: places	Proper nouns: things	Titles used with names (President Lincoln)	Abbreviations	Titles of books, magazines	Days and months	First word of direct quotation

Class Record-Keeping Grid: Commas

	Items in a series	After a signal word at the begin of sentence	To separate person talking from rest of sentence	Sentence opener, then a comma	To separate clauses	To separate month and year in a date	In greeting and closing in a letter

Class Record-Keeping Grid: Rules of Dialogue

	1) Place quotation marks around the exact words of the speaker.	2) Capitalize the first word of a direct quotation.	3) Include end punctuation marks, sometimes a comma, inside the quotation marks.	4) Identify the speaker.	*Use alternatives for the overused verb *said*.

APPENDIX: STUDENT WRITING SAMPLES

To print out these reproducibles at full size, please visit www.scholastic.com/masteringthemechanics.

Paulina

If I were the Queen

If I where the queen bee. I would live with alot of other bees. I would need to get my food from other bees. They take care of me. I would lay alot of eggs every day I would be the only queen. I would live for three years. The other bees would keep me warm dering the winter. I would use my stinger to kill other queens I would eat Speshil food to turn into a queen. The end

stinger stringer stinggor

Megan H
June 6

How to make a bed

1. First be prepared with the clean
sheets.

2. Next, take off all the covers
and sheets, including pillowcases
off the bed.

elastic corner

3. Then make sure that the bottom
fitted sheet is going the
right direction. Put the sheet
on with the long side going down
the bed, and pull the corners
so that everything is smooth.

4 in.

4. Take the top sheet and place it
on the bed so that the same
amount of sheet hangs on
each side. The top should
be folded really about 4 inches.
On the bottom end of the bed the
sheet will hang down a lot.

bottom first, then fold and push in

5. Push in the corners so that
it looks like the ___ corner
of a envelop.

6. Put the cases on or 7. Add on the bed case.
8. Add pillows on.

Hip Hip Hooray

We were getting our math tests back and Jose said "Yea! I got an A, I only missed one!" Some kids had there tests back but I was still waiting. I was saying to myself "you just have to get an A. You just have to get an A!" "Please get an A!"

My stomack was in a knott when Mrs.C finally set it down. "YES!!!" I gave a quiet cheer. I was sooooo releeved.

stomack
stomeck
stomauk

Micàel leaned over and wispered "way to go! Then Mrs.C called "Class. May I have your atention please." The class still as a butterfly's wings.

atention
~~atension~~

With our eyes on Mrs.C she smiled ~~said~~ "Everyone did so well we're playing math games for the last 15 minuts of class" "Congratulation".

We cheered, "Hip Hip Hooray" 3 times for mrs C. Math was really fun that day!!!

The Noise   #30
                    KAtlynn

I was walking rite around the hall
conner. When I heard a Noise It wasent
a Scarry Noise it Sounded like Nails chraching
on a chalk Bord, it heart My eyndrum's.
So I walked in and gess what I found
a chere wh,th Brown hair and razer sharp
teeth and ugly weab feet, But all I Know
whas that it loked Mad. and it Smelled
like a a garbg truck, I wonder what it
tastis like But I took no chances, it looked
wet Scally and hairy. So I Dicied to Call it
Mister Nastie, this animal looked mean, I
caled it that Because it ate My class
Bunny. I dent know what to Do So
I ran to go and tell a teacher But I
could not find enyone so I ran in to
the class and knoked the chiner out

The Noise • © 2008 Hoyt & Therriault • Scholastic • Mastering the Mechanics: Grades 4-5

Tim W.
6th hr.
June 9th

The Feeasco ⑤

⟨3⟩ Today is my first day ~~of~~ to be the
assisstant
~~assisstant~~ coach for my little brother's soccer
team. He's in kindergarten. My science
teacher talked me into it. It sounded like a
GREAT idea a month a go but now that the
                           not
day ~~has~~ come I'm ~~wasn't~~ so sure; For one
                   has
thing the dog dragged ~~Martiin's~~ Max's soccer clothes out
threw the doggie door so its time to go and
his stuff is all over the backyard.

     When we ~~finetly~~ got there I barely
              finaly
made it. ~~Any~~ The coach Mr. A's eyebrows raised up.
That meant Yourd late! Anyway Mr.A's voice got
                  almost
loud the kid's voices got quite. Then 5 of the
kid's were mine. They stood there ~~giggling~~! ⑤
                                   giggling
and moving. All I could think was so now
what?

The Fiasco • © 2008 Hoyt & Therriault • Scholastic • *Mastering the Mechanics: Grades 4–5*

Teresa
#17

The Storm of the century
~~Extreme storms~~

    If you believe that the storm of the century was a blizzard, you'd be ~~wo~~ wrong. If you guessed tornado or flood, you'd still be wrong. But, if you guessed it was a combination of all three, blizzard, tornado, and flood you'd be right on.

    The storm was called a nor'easter. That's when winds blow, really blow, from north-east, especially along the United States' northeast coast.

    ~~this~~ The year was 1993 when the nor'easter hit from Maine to Florida. It closed down ~~every airport~~ most airports on the eastern coast. It dumped snow ~~from~~ and caused about 50 tornadoes.

The Storm of the Century • © 2008 Hoyt & Therriault • Scholastic • Mastering the Mechanics: Grades 4-5

1. Reminder | Use your helping verb list
2. Pick out 1 main verb
3. Add helping verbs
4. Go!

April 17

Main Verb = action + Helping

I shall walk.
I may walk.
I should walk
I must walk
I would walk but
I could walk
I will walk
I can walk
I did walk
I do walk
I have walked
I am walking.
I was walking.
I had

I have been walks in the park.
I shall be walks in the park.
I had been
I must have walked at least.

I will have walked.

I shall

2½ min.

Quick Write

Robbie and I had been walking for hours. We had crossed a raging creek about an hour ago, but now we weren't certain where we were. We retraced our steps by closely looking at our map. Finally, after what seemed like a long time but was probably only several minutes, we located our position on the map.

I should take notes I muttered. Robbie agreed I was busy taking note when the rest of our party came into sight! YES! We could walk out with the rest of our group and we would enjoy the hike back without worrying. We must try this again without getting lost. 31

Cecelia

<u>Your's, Mine, and Our's</u>

My sister and me share a bedroom. Sometimes its great to have a roommate and other times its horendous (SP). We came up with a way to stop are fighting. Its called "Your's, Mine, and Our's". Our parent's bought us our own dressers. Now we have our own sides of the room too. We share a work table, but we each have our own box of supplys

Now we just need to keep our little brother out that's easier said then done !!

Eddie #2

Ms. G.

1-31

Afterschool

Afterschool I like to play football with my dad. We play for a long time until we get bored. I sometimes play with a sponge ball that you could throw over 100 yards, but it's hard to catch, and sometimes when were playing in the dark you just have to stick out your hands and hope you catch it but sometimes it will hit you in the head. It doesn't hurt though, because it made of sponge. Once I was playing in the dark and I I threw the ball about 60 yards and hit him in the face,

A Bum Rap
By B. B. Wolf

I may be known as the Big Bad Wolf (B.B. for short). But I got a bum rap and I am here to tell you how it really went down…

Slowly strolling along, my brother Al and I were out exercising his pet pig, Porkie. My brother he likes pigs a lot so he has always got a few of them wandering around in his yard for company. As we meandered along minding our own business, this really bossy mama pig comes raging up and demands that we come and help her kids. She says they are trapped in their house and need someone to help get them out.

Quickly, me and my brother grabbed Porkie and went racing to the pigs' house. Just like that bossy mama said, there were three pig faces in the window looking scared as can be and the door was stuck tight.

With a huge puff of shared wolf-power my brother and I we huffed and we puffed and we blew as hard as we could. Sure enough that house blew down and there sat three confused looking little pigs.

You can imagine how surprised we were when the police came roaring up and threw Al and me in jail.

Proper Tooth Care...A MUST!!!

By David S. and Carolyn H.

Do you want false teeth when you get old? Do you want root canals when your not even old? If you don't start taking better care of your teeth these could be your future!

Kids' teeth should be in much better shape than they are. We interviewed kindergartens through fifth graders and your mouth would fall open and hit the ground if you heard what we heard!!

Four out of every five kids went to bed WITHOUT brushing their teeth at least one night every week. Just think. All those germs spending a 10 hour recess in your mouth just wrecking your teeths' chance for a good healthy life.

Even MORE alarming (we only checked with the 4th and 5th graders on this question) only one in 10 kids flossed! The dentists' opinion is that this is extremely important to get rid of plaque, which causes tooth decay too.

We didn't even ask kids if they were eating junk food, we just watched and almost everybody did. We know that we should eat better, more fruits, vegetables, and less candy. This will help our teeth.

So eat better foods, brush and floss every night if you want your teeth to last. Remember, an ounce of prevention is worth a pound of cure!

Proper Tooth Care…A MUST! • © 2008 Hoyt & Therriault • Scholastic • *Mastering the Mechanics: Grades 4–5*

A True American Hero
The Story of Rosa Parks

She wasn't a tall woman or a loud woman. She wasn't a woman who made a scene. She was a tired woman, riding a bus, heading home after a long days work.

As the bus filled up, Rosa Parks sat quietly, until the bus drive told her that she needed to give up her seat to a white man. He expected this quiet black woman to follow his order, figuring that no black person would face jail just for a bus seat. He was wrong.

Mrs. Parks decided to stand up for her rights by remaining seated. She was arrested and went to trial. But this quiet lady, Dr. Martin Luther King, and thousands of others changed America forever. They did it without violence. They had a dream and followed it. Mrs. Rosa Parks is a TRUE American hero. I thank you.

A True American Hero • © 2008 Hoyt & Therriault • Scholastic • *Mastering the Mechanics: Grades 4–5*

By Darby

Penguin Bodys

Penguins are not your ordinarey birds. There feathers may look like fur, but thy are, in fact, feathers. There mostly black on top and white on there bellies. From the sky, the black looks like the bottom of the water and from below, there white bellies look like ice or jest blend with the sky.

Most other birds use there feathers to fly. Not the penguins. Thay can't fly but are good simmers. There long, outer feathers help keep the water out. Under the outer feathers is a layer of down. Anuther layer comes below the down. However, its not feathers, but blubber. The blubber helps them stay warm in the cold waters of Antarctica. Most birds wuoldn't want to live there.

Short legs are set back on there bodys. This makes them sway back and forth when they walk. Some call this waddling. Thay look awkward on land. This is one reason why thay slide on there bellys. Once thay dive into the sea, there good divers, thay become gracefull.

Investigating a Crime

Most of Watching T.V.

Crime Investigations

More efficiently checking clues and evidence

Abruptly sealing off the crime scene

Yucker! But the finger prints

Samples. Yucker! Now glove

Never let the criminal go

Always give the important

Investigating a Crime

Head Lice

I have this teacher. She is really nice. But some time I think she has head lice. She itches all day. And the last time for head lice check she got sent home from school. I would tell you more but it is not cool. The day she came back she had no hair and her head was bear. I think to my self how did she get the lice. I kept on thinking until I new that I was not nice because I'm the one who gave her the lice.

By: Samantha

Head Lice • © 2008 Hoyt & Therriault • Scholastic • *Mastering the Mechanics: Grades 4–5*

A Harry Potter Book Review by Carlos M.

My favorite author is JK Rowling. Everyone knows she has written the Harry Potter books. She teaches us lessons about life and entertains us. I think she does a good job of developing her characters. Even Harry isn't perfect all the time. I've had some of his problems with friends and schoolwork.

I am reading the fifth book, Order Of The Phoenix. If I was JK, I would have written these chapter titles:" The Order Begins", "Kids on a Mission", "Lessons Learned", and " Fighting for Justice". I won't tell you which chapters they go with. You'll need to read the book and make a guess. Then will I let you know!

Anyone want to have a Harry Potter book club? Let me know. I love to talk about Harry!

A Harry Potter Book Review • © 2008 Hoyt & Therriault • Scholastic • *Mastering the Mechanics: Grades 4–5*

The Heart

With unrelenting consistency, the muscles of the heart squeeze together. These contractions of the heart are so powerful they could send a jet of water six feet high into the air. Each time the muscles contract, blood surges through the chambers of the heart gathering speed, pulsing with power. As the blood pushes out of the left ventricle of the heart, it smashes with great force into the aorta, the blood vessel that directs blood away from the heart and toward the rest of the body. Deep and fast, blood streams into ever-smaller tunnels. Shivery and quick, blood travels into veins and capillaries delivering oxygen and nutrients to needy cells.

The Heart • © 2008 Hoyt & Therriault • Scholastic • Mastering the Mechanics: Grades 4–5

Arthropods: The Crayfish

The crayfish has a fairly complicated nervous system that helps it control movement as well as its senses. The system runs the entire length of the body with a ganglion, a small localized "brain," controlling each segment of the body. A collection of ganglion. The head region has many ganglion that control the others around the body.

Arthropods: The Crayfish • © 2008 Hoyt & Therriault • Scholastic • Mastering the Mechanics: Grades 4–5

BIBLIOGRAPHY

Anderson, J. (2005). *Mechanically inclined: Building grammar, usage, and style into writer's workshop.* Portland, ME: Stenhouse.

Angelillo, J. (2002). *A fresh approach to teaching punctuation: Helping young writers use conventions with precision and purpose.* New York: Scholastic.

Calkins, L. & Louis, N. (2003). *Writing for readers: Teaching skills and strategies.* Portsmouth, NH: Heinemann.

Culham, R. (2003). *6+1 traits of writing: The complete guide: Grades 3 and up.* New York: Scholastic.

Department of Education, Western Australia. (2006). *Writing map of development* (2nd ed.).

Fletcher, R. & Portalupi, J. (2001). *Writing workshop: The essential guide.* Portsmouth, NH: Heinemann.

Graves, D. (1994). *A fresh look at writing.* Portsmouth, NH: Heinemann.

Harwayne, S. (2001). *Writing through childhood: Rethinking process and product.* Portsmouth, NH: Heinemann.

Harwayne, S. (1992). *Lasting impressions: Weaving literature into the writing workshop.* Portsmouth, NH: Heinemann.

Ray, K. W. (1999). *Wonderous words.* Portsmouth, NH: Heinemann.

Ray, K. W. & Cleaveland, L. (2004). *About the authors: Writing workshop with our youngest writers.* Portsmouth, NH: Heinemann.

Routman, R. (2004). *Writing essentials: Raising expectations and results while simplifying teaching.* Portsmouth, NH: Heinemann.

Sitton, R. (2006). *Rebecca Sitton's sourcebook for teaching spelling and word skills.* Scottsdale, AZ: Egger Publishing, Inc.

Taylor, B. M., Pearson, P. D., Peterson, D. S., & Rodriguez, M. C. (2002). Looking inside classrooms: Reflecting on the "how" as well as the "what" in effective reading instruction. *The Reading Teacher, 56* (3), 270–279.

Topping, D. H. & Hoffman, S. J. (2006). *Getting grammar: 150 new ways to teach an old subject.* Portsmouth, NH: Heinemann.

INDEX